SHAPING A HEALTHY RELIGION
ESPECIALLY IF YOU ARE CATHOLIC

SHAPING A HEALTHY RELIGION
ESPECIALLY IF YOU ARE CATHOLIC

Thomas Aldworth, O.F.M.

THE THOMAS MORE PRESS
Chicago, Illinois

CONTENTS

Preface

THE title, *Shaping a Healthy Religion Especially If You Are Catholic,* is not intended as any comment upon Catholicism. Being Catholic makes a healthy religion neither harder nor easier. All religions have their flaws. But since I am Catholic, I am more familiar with the ways Catholism helps and hinders healthy religion. If I were a Buddhist, then the ending of the title would be "Especially if You're Buddhist." The same hold true for being Moslem, Jewish, or whatever.

Catholicism can certainly help one discover God. It can also get in the way of such a discovery. Catholicism can certainly help one to develop her or his full humanity. It can also retard such development. Many of the things I have to say might seem critical of the church. I'm afraid I don't spend a great deal of time on all the ways the church has helped me to grow. I apologize in advance. The church is vitally important to me. I pray that my examination is done in love, for without love there can be no faith.

Chapter One
IMAGES OF GOD

ALL of us have memories of childhood. Those of us who were raised Catholic will have many memories of what church meant to us. Some will be funny. Some will be sad. Some will help us in our quest for understanding and meaning. Some will be unpleasant. I would like to begin with a memory which continues to give me comfort, even after almost twenty-five years. I had just finished serving the midnight Christmas mass at our church. I was walking home alone. I was just twelve years old and my father had died a few months previously. I was thinking of my father and thinking about God as I made my way home. There was a light snow falling. All was quiet. I began to sense a feeling of peace which held me in its embrace and made me oblivious to the cold. I knew that the feeling had something to do with the Christmas mass and also with my father and also with God. I have never forgotten that feeling. It encouraged me to consider priesthood.

So I left my home at the age of thirteen to enter the minor seminary. For the next thirteen years, I studied and learned what I would need to know upon ordination. Finally, in 1974, I was ordained as a Franciscan priest. Since then I have spent my years in various ministries. I've seen some of the ways in which religion is healthy and some of the ways in which it is not.

Naturally, I'm a believer in religion. I wouldn't be in this profession otherwise. I believe religion can help us grow into loving and fully human people. I also believe religion can keep us in various kinds of prisons. So let's examine some of the thoughts, practices, and rituals which are part of the Catholic religion. Many of these thoughts, however, could easily be extended to other Christian denominations. Healthy religion is something most of us seek.

I was born and raised on the South Side of Chicago, in one of those neighborhoods where it seemed that everyone was Catholic. I knew only one Protestant child. He lived next door to us. I remember feeling sad that he wouldn't be able to get to heaven. We all knew heaven was reserved for Catholics. At least that's how the message of salvation came across to me. I was glad to be Catholic. God belonged to us. After all, didn't he send his son to start the Catholic Church?

We weren't raised to dislike non-Catholics, it's just we didn't trust them. For instance, the only swimming pool in my neighborhood was at the local YMCA. But we couldn't go swimming there because we might become "tainted." I remember thinking Protestant children probably leaked something into the water which would make me less able to defend my faith. We weren't ordered not to swim at the Y, but it was suggested that it was a dangerous thing to do. I didn't learn to swim until I was in college.

The church is very important to me. I care deeply about her. She has nourished me and given me a world view. But as I grew in age and understanding, it became clear that some of this world view was distorted. So I have had to do an inventory, keeping what was good and discarding what was not. Yet I will always remain within the structure of the church. It's a part of me. To deny it would be like denying I'm Irish. It's the ground from which I grew. Yet the church does have blemishes. To cover them over or ignore them doesn't promote healing.

We all know mothers who have no other identity except motherhood. The church is often like that. We even speak of her as "Mother Church." And, like many mothers, the church tries to keep her children as children. She doesn't do this maliciously. Maybe she's afraid. Many mothers fear their children growing up and leaving home. Maybe the church doesn't believe her children can grow up and still love her. The uncertainty about her children's love can make her uneasy. Meanwhile, her children grow up uncertain how to both love the church and become an adult.

Part of the problem is that Christianity is difficult, if not impossible, to teach to children. The ideas Jesus taught have to do with letting go of our ego, our conception of ourself. Jesus' teaching makes little sense to children, who do not yet have fully formed ideas of who they are. So what happens is we give our children the Old Testament notions of God. We teach them the stories of Adam and Eve, Noah and the Ark, Moses and the Ten Commandments. The children, not having the intellectual growth needed to understand what myth is, come to accept these stories as historically true. When that happens, they begin to have an unhealthy view of God.

Now I don't wish to get into a long debate about the Old Testament stories. There have been many books written on understanding the Old Testament. But I do want to say that while these stories have a message, a theological truth, many of them were not intended to express history. The stories, especially the earlier stories, present myth. Myth is a way we handle mysteries which are beyond our scientific and rational capabilities. Myth is important in religion. It presents a message. The trouble occurs when we mistake myth for history. They are not the same.

Our young people in high school are being taught some of these ideas about the Old Testament stories. This often leads to conflicts. Many of them really did believe that Adam and Eve existed. When they are told such stories are mythical, they often begin to distrust everything they were taught in religion. They feel that they were lied to for so many years. It's like when we first learn that Santa Claus is not real.

What the high-school students are taught also creates family crises. They come home from school and tell the rest of the family what they have learned. Many parents feel themselves unable to adequately respond. Parents may claim that the teachers don't know what they're talking about, which makes the young person have to choose whom to believe. Parents may feel let down by the church. They may begin to have some religious doubts of their own. In short, the situation becomes an unhealthy one. It's not that doubts are in themselves unhealthy. Doubts have a place in healthy religion. What is unhealthy is to have families fragmented because of faulty or inadequate religious teaching.

The Old Testament portrayal of God is important, but it must be seen as a stage in our religious understanding. In the Old Testament, God is often pictured as too small, too vindictive, too violent. The conceptualization, the experience, of God does broaden as we progress through the Old Testament. But when we give our children their first picture of God, it is often from the early stages of the Old Testament. Take the story of Adam and Eve. They were banished from the Garden after eating from the tree of good and evil. The reason they are banished is because God's afraid. He's afraid they might eat from the tree of life and live forever. Therefore, God puts an angel with a flaming sword at the entrance to bar any return. What we have then is a story picturing God as being jealous of immortality. He doesn't want to share it. We also have God walking around the Garden, trying to cool himself. We have Eve being commanded to be submissive to Adam. These things make God appear foolish. He's pictured as possessing all our human traits.

Take the story of Noah and the Ark. It's possible there may have been a flood of some type which served as the starting point for this story. The story may also have been taken from the Babylonian myth, *The Gilgamesh Epic*. But regardless where the story comes from, what does it say about God? We have a God who gets angry with what he has created. Humanity is sinful so God decides to destroy them all. He relents a bit and saves Noah and his family, along with different pairs of animals (not just the one pair as is usually portrayed).

Now what kind of God would wipe out everything he has created? Since God is portrayed as knowing the future, why would he have created man and the animals, knowing he would destroy them? Why would God kill all the animals, except for a chosen few? Were the animals also sinners? Couldn't God have destroyed humanity without also destroying all other life as well? What we get in the story of Noah and the Ark is a destroying, angry God. It's a horrible portrayal. Could we possibly believe that God is a loving father when he is also prone to fits of cataclysmic rage?

The Old Testament Israelites believed that God was their God alone. They also believed he would be on their side in battle. The Old Testament is filled with stories about the Israelites wiping out their enemies and giving God the credit. Whenever they conquered a city or town, they would destroy every living thing in it. Women, children, animals were all destroyed to appease the God who had given them the victory. They also worshiped God by sacrificing goats, sheep, and other animals by the thousands. What kind of God would wish total destruction after victory? What kind of God would like to see his creation slaughtered? Not a God worth believing in.

Imagine what these ideas do to our children. They see God as someone to fear. How can they respond any differently? The Old Testament stories do little justice to God. We can learn from them, to be sure, but we must be very careful when we use them with our children. Otherwise, they will see all the destruction laid at God's feet and begin to fear God. They will be afraid that God will "get them" if they're not good.

Scripture speaks of "fear of the Lord" as the beginning of wisdom. But Scripture is speaking about a sense of reverence, a response based on humility. It's not speaking about fearing God the way we fear stormy nights or dark alleys. If we're afraid of God, we'll try to hide from him. It's like being in a classroom when we haven't studied. We try to make ourselves as inconspicuous as we can so the teacher won't call on us. If we're afraid of God, we try not to be noticed. I remember as a child, hiding in a closet during a thunderstorm. I thought God was trying to get me for fighting with my twin brother. The lightning was surely meant for me. When I wasn't incinerated, I figured God was either giving me another chance or he was a bad shot.

There are, of course, some teachers and parents who like having their children afraid of God. Then God can be used like a paddle to correct behavior. What better way to have a child pay attention than to have him or her threatened with "God will get you if you don't behave"? Is it any wonder, then, why so many of our young people reject the notion of God when they get the chance? If God has been used against them, if God has been on the side of their parents, can they have a healthy notion of God?

A healthy religion for children implies a healthy

religion already existing in the parents. If a child's parents have a good and healthy conception of God, the child will be able to grow in his or her religion. The opposite is also true. Our conception of God is tied to our mental health. If a child's parent's are healthy psychologically, they will be more capable of passing on to their children a healthy religion. Again the opposite is also true.

The experience of one's parents often relates to one's conceptualization of God. As M. Scott Peck points out in his book, *The Road Less Traveled*: "Our first (and sadly, often our only) notion of God's nature is a simple extrapolation of our parents' natures, a simple blending of the characters of our mothers and fathers or their substitutes. If we have loving, forgiving parents, we are likely to believe in a loving, forgiving God. . . . If our parents were harsh and punitive, we are likely to mature with a concept of a harsh and punitive monster-god."

This doesn't mean that we can't grow in our understanding of God. The problem is that many of us continue to accept the religious ideas we were given as children. We stay with our childish notions, or we give up on God altogether. Often, as we grow, we see that many of the things we were taught need to be redefined. But it's a tragedy to throw out belief in God, instead of merely discarding our childish notions of him. Our understanding and awareness of God must develop as we develop. Otherwise, we are like adults wearing children's clothes. Often the Catholic Church is seen as having too much time and effort invested in children's clothes.

A child's world is a world concerned with rewards and punishments. Children are naturally selfish, which is a necessary stage of growth. "Give me" is the overwhelming refrain of childhood. So the God who makes sense to children is one who appears very much like Santa Claus. God will reward us when we are good and punish us when we are bad. Santa will bring presents if we are good, and he will bring a lump of coal if we are bad. God will give us heaven or send us to hell.

Just as we must be careful with the idea of Santa Claus, so we must be careful with the idea of God as one who rewards and punishes. Santa Claus is a notion very dear to American hearts. God as rewarder and punisher is very dear to some religions' hearts. I discovered how dear we hold Santa while I was in a parish in Parma, Ohio. I was teaching in the first grade, just before Christmas, when one of the children asked me if I believed in Santa Claus. I knew I was in trouble. I knew that some of the children still believed in him. Yet I also knew I couldn't claim belief in Santa. So I told the children that the idea of Santa Claus helped make Christmas fun but he wasn't real. By the look on some children's faces, I knew my answer wasn't good enough.

The rectory's phones began ringing not long afterwards. Obviously agitated parents were accusing me of destroying Christmas. Now it's certainly true that my timing was unfortunate. I could probably have handled the question in a more delicate way. Anyway, I tried to explain to the callers the reasons for my opposition to Santa Claus. The premise of Santa is that if you're good, you get presents; if you're bad, you don't. But what about those good children who happen to belong to poor families? If Johnny down the street gets twice as many presents as Sally, does that make Johnny twice as good? I also believe children suffer some damage when they learn their parents lied about Santa Claus. Children need to believe in the integrity of their parents.

Anyway, I became known as the grump who stole Christmas. But because of the debate, I began to see more clearly how a child's view of God is often interrelated with ideas like Santa Claus. As children, we begin to think God's favor is something we must win, just as we must be good to get lots of Christmas presents. God will not like us if we are bad. We imagine God's love to be conditional. Just as parents might seem to withdraw their love from a naughty child, so God might withdraw his love in the same way. Just as parents will paddle children when they misbehave, so God will keep track of all misdeeds and make sure punishment is meted out.

We don't help our children when we present God as someone who rewards and punishes. If God exists, which I believe, then he must love us no matter what we do. If I beat up my little brother, God still loves me. If I steal something from the store, God still loves me. If I disobey my mother or father, God still loves me. It's this notion of God's unceasing love which must be handed on to our children. Anything less creates an image of God which is too small. A healthy religion is centered on this notion of God's never-ending love.

It's difficult to teach children about God. There are many treacherous twists and turns on the road. We must be careful where we begin. If we start with the early Old Testament pictures of God, we are already in a mine field. If we just open the Bible and take the images from Genesis, we'll be starting in the wrong place. Children need to first understand that God is a personal force within the universe. The force, to use St. John's terminology, is love. When we feel love either for or from someone, then God is present to us. Children can understand love if there is love in their lives. What they know about love will be limited, but it's a good starting place. They can understand God as the Spirit of Love living in our world. We can still use the Old Testament truth that God is the Creator but we must be cautious how we present such a truth.

Almost all children have seen the movie *Star Wars* or its sequels. It might be helpful to talk of God in terms of "The Force." Not that God and "The Force" are the same thing. Yet similarities could be shown to the children. God is a loving force, filling the universe. In the movie, a dark side of "The Force" is also spoken about. We could speak of evil as the dark side of "The Force." Now I hope I don't get accused of promoting a *Star Wars* theology. Yet I think that some of the ideas of *Star Wars* would be more helpful to children than some of the ideas of the Old Testament.

Most children, if you ask them to describe God, will picture him as a man with a long white beard, sitting on a cloud somewhere. William B. Silverman notes the results of such a survey in his *God Help Me!*: "Between 70 and 80 percent of the children believed that God has a face, hands, and feet like a man." But if our children think of God only in bodily terms, they will get confused about the true nature of God. How can God be everywhere if he has hands and feet like us? The universe is considered to be at least 12 billion light years across. With light traveling at 186,000 miles a second, that makes for a very large universe! And God must be everywhere in that universe if he is God. He must be at least as large as the universe. If he's thought of as sitting on a cloud somewhere, we again wind up with a God who's too small.

There's another problem with believing that God has a body like ours. A child knows that two bodies can't occupy the same space. If we want to sit in a chair that's already occupied by our brother or sister, there's a conflict. How can a child visualize living within God, if God has a body like ours? And because we sometimes think of God as having such a body, we put him in a place called heaven. If God has a body, then he must "live" somewhere. God, as body, gets relegated to a place apart from us.

Children need to understand that they live inside of God. To try and get this idea across, I will sometimes bring a fish and small fish-tank into the classroom. I ask the children what would happen if the fish were taken from the water. Most know that the fish would die. They also know that we need the air around us to breathe or we would be like fish without water. I go on to explain that it's the same way with

God. If we didn't live within him, then we could never love. Fish need water to live. We need air to live. We need God to love. And we live in God like the fish lives in the water. This idea of living in God is hard to imagine if we see God in bodily terms.

We have, throughout history, also thought of God in masculine terminology. It's difficult to think of God only as a loving Spirit. But before the idea of one God, humans fashioned gods of all types to describe their experience of mystery. Dennis Geaney points this out in *Living with Your Conscience*: "Since the first grey dawn of human consciousness, man has made God to his own image and likeness, that is, his understanding of who God is has been fashioned from human experience. God not only ordered the universe, but in the minds of men he was quite capricious and arbitrary. He hurled bolts of lightning, stoked the fires that ravished the lands, stirred the waves in his temper tantrums that would demolish the works of man on land or at sea or withhold the water from crops until man would come to terms with his sinfulness." What we have done throughout history is bestow divinity upon things we either didn't understand or feared.

There have been many gods and goddesses who have made their way into our religious history. The Egyptians had Isis, Osiris, and Re. The Babylonians had Marduk and Tiamat. The Canaanites had Baal, Astarte, and El. The Greeks had Athena, Poseidon, Apollo, and Zeus. The Romans had Juno, Minerva, Mars, and Jupiter. The Irish had Brigit and Dagda. The Germanic peoples had Odin and Thor. The list goes on and on. It is almost impossible to keep track of them all.

It was the Israelites who first came to believe in one God. People up to that time believed in many gods and goddesses. The Israelites, at first, believed that there were other gods but they only worshiped their one God, who was stronger than any other god. It was he who brought them out of slavery in Egypt. It was he who led them into the "Promised Land." He was their God. They belonged to him and he belonged to them. With time and the help of the prophets, however, the Israelites began to see that their God was the God of everyone. There was but one God.

The Israelites' history is the gradual unfolding and understanding of the nature of God. We call this unfolding "salvation history." When Jesus comes, he brings a new flash of understanding. So we can have a much healthier view of God than the ancients, due to the attempts of the Israelites to understand, coupled with the insights of Jesus. We should not, however, dismiss our pagan heritage altogether. Their sense of the sacred, their awe before the mysterious can help us to know what it means to live in wonder. Certainly there were pagan excesses. Uncounted masses were sacrificed to appease some god or goddess. Thousands at a time lost their lives on the altar of the Aztec sun god, Tonatiuh. Yet through the study of all religions, past as well as present, we will see more clearly the roads which dead-end and those which lead somewhere. It is the impulse to worship that demands our study, not always what was worshiped.

Surely the ancients experienced God. It was in their descriptions of him that they often went astray. Whenever we attempt to define God, we run into trouble. Yet words and definitions are what we use to communicate. If I experience the holy, I will want to share that experience with those who are close to me. But my definition will leave much to be desired. My words will fall short. They will mirror the experience only dimly. Meister Eckhart, a fourteenth century Dominican mystic, realized this when he pointed out that God is much more what we don't say about him than what we do say.

Sometimes our descriptions of God get in the way of our experience of him. It's difficult for us to broaden our definitions, our visualizations. Look at the idea of God as "Father." I remember preaching one day at my first parish in Quincy, Illinois. I mentioned that while we normally speak of God as "Father," he also mothers us. I said God could be spoken of as "Mother" as well as "Father." The sermon didn't have the desired result. Its message was conveyed to the bishop in Springfield. I realized the need for caution.

Now Jesus had a human body and he continues to have it. Jesus was and is God. Jesus was and is fully human. But to say that Jesus shares in Godhood does not make God human. When we speak of God as "Father" we need to be careful not to fashion him in paternal terms. God does "father" us. But God also "mothers" us. He "brothers" us. He "sisters" us. He befriends us. What we say, ultimately, is that God "loves" us. And since there are many ways to understand love, so there are many ways to understand what God does to us.

It's all right to speak of God as "Father" in the sense that God gives life and calls us to grow. Yet a mother also gives us life and calls us to grow. Perhaps we could speak of "masculine" and "feminine" sides of God. In the early church, there were theologians who spoke of the Holy Spirit in feminine terms, and if we are going to speak about God at all we need some analogies. Analogies are what we use when we want to compare. God is *like* a father. God is *like* a mother. Yet all analogies are said to limp. We need to remember that when we use terms to describe God. He is a father to us, but he is much more than a father.

So how can we help our children understand God? If we only speak of God in parental terms, then we may be doing a disservice to them. They may make God into a "Superparent." As George Anderson states in his *Your Religion: Healthy or Neurotic?*: "Religion provides us with a God upon whom we often project the qualities of our unconscious idealized mother or father. We bind ourselves, or relate to God, as we would to our mother or father." And while our relationship with our parents colors every other relationship, God needs to be connected more with the notion of love than parenthood.

Perhaps the concepts found in the First Letter of St. John would be a better starting point for our children than the Book of Genesis. God as light; God as love; these images can be conveyed even to our smallest students. Once these concepts are communicated, we could begin to tell the story of how people came to know God. We could tell the children that God is the Creator, having made everything. But we would also have to tell the children that we aren't sure how God made everything. The Genesis account is only one attempt to explain. We would also want to present what science has to say about creation. The important thing being taught is that God is the Creator, even if we're not sure how he did it.

The experience of life brings questions. Children are filled with such questions. It was the same with the Israelites. They had questions about life and their experience of God. They attempted to answer the questions through the Old Testament. The Old Testament is a written account of the searching that took place within the minds, hearts, and souls of the Israelites. Some of the answers they came up with are wonderful. Some are not. Their world view, their vocabulary, their knowledge structured their answers. Since we today possess more knowledge, we would fashion different answers. Many answers are possible to the questions of life and God.

Scripture was not intended to be a history book as we know the term. It presents history, but from a subjective viewpoint. When the Israelites won a victory, they naturally assumed their God was stronger than the gods or gods of the vanquished. If they lost the battle, they believed God could have won, but he must be punishing them for some reason. It was a simple world view. It answered a lot of questions. But it was just one interpretation for what happened. There could be many others. Many of the Old Testament stories have a theological message which is still valid, but we must be careful when we present the message. Children need to see that it's the message which is important, not the wrapping.

I do not believe that Scripture is literally true. It's not accurate in many respects. There are a good number of people, however, who do believe Scripture word for word. They are sometimes spoken of as "fundamentalists." Holding such a literal view of Scripture has drawbacks. For instance, if we build a world according to the first chapter of Genesis, we have a flat world, covered with a dome, with gates to let in the rain. And what about the mark of Cain? There have been some throughout history who have used the mark of Cain as a racist weapon. But let's look at the story. Cain kills his brother Abel because God, for no apparent reason, rejects the sacrifice of Cain in favor of the offering of Abel. God then puts a mark on Cain's forehead to prevent all the other people in the world from killing him. But if Cain and Abel are the two sons of Adam and Eve, where did all the other people come from? Yet these stories never intended to present history. They were intended to convey messages and truths. We can understand the truth of the Cain and Abel story: Violence is born into the world because of rejection.

Many times the stories were written to account for something already existing. The story of the tower of Babel, for instance, was used to explain how language diversified. The story was invented to explain what had already occurred. It was also a sarcastic comment upon the high towers, or Ziggurats, of the Babylonians. Another example would be the story of Lot's wife being turned into a pillar of salt. The story helps explain why the Dead Sea has so much salt in it. Lot's wife met her fateful end on the shores of the Dead Sea. The connections are often quite poetic.

If we hold to a literal interpretation, we run into many problems. The biggest problem is with the kind of God portrayed in many of the stories. I was taught as a child to believe in such a literal scriptural interpretation. Most of us were probably raised the same way. This view of Scripture has kept many of us from gaining a healthy view of God. As Silverman says in *God Help Me!*: "The fundamental approach is a sincere but futile attempt to justify the Divine authority of Holy Scripture as irrefutable and unalterable. In essence, it is religious blasphemy and scathing indictment of a God of love."

This is still a very difficult area for people. I have more than once preached about Adam and Eve. I have tried to point out the theological message and the question with which the story is grappling. If God is perfect, how did his creation wind up so imperfect? The story of Adam and Eve was created to answer the question. Yet if you tell people Adam and Eve didn't exist, except as symbols, some take it hard. They believe you're attacking something central to the faith, even though the historicity of Adam and Eve is not very important.

Many of us, however, were raised to construct a

belief system with Old Testament stories as the core. We become frightened if the accuracy of the stories is challenged. Some of us may claim that if the facts of the stories are doubted, then we are doubting God. I've come across this belief a number of times. One summer I was working in clinical pastoral training at a Southern Baptist hospital in San Antonio. A couple of the Baptists in the program felt a person couldn't be a Christian if they didn't hold to Scripture literally. We had some lively discussions that summer.

In virtually every seminary and theology school where people study for the priesthood, they will be taught how to interpret Scripture. Catholic Scriptural studies have come a very long way in the past hundred years. Yet these new understandings don't always get to the people in the parish. Some priests may be hesitant about preaching a nonliteral view of Scripture. The furor that can be raised often makes even strong-hearted priests a bit reluctant. Most priests don't want to "stir up" their people. Many, as pictured in the play *Mass Appeal,* would rather be liked by their parishioners than tread on potentially taboo ground. And who can fault them? All of us who are priests have a need for human affirmation and affection. We may even need more of it than most. Yet the dilemma remains. Priests and all who teach religion must help their people form a healthy religion. Anything harmful to healthy religion must be exposed. I believe a literal view of Scripture is harmful. It needs to be replaced with an understanding of the struggles which Scripture embodies.

I'd like to end this first section by saying that the Old Testament view of God is often too small, too vindictive, too petty, and too cruel. But that doesn't rule out recognizing how Scripture broadens its view of God as it progresses. It moves from a childish understanding to a more mature understanding. We must move in a similar way. We need to move from the view of God we received as children to a more mature view.

How we think about God affects our experience of him. If he is seen as a kindly old man, sitting on a cloud some place, then we have too great a separation between us. God is closer to us than we are to ourselves. But original sin (and not the kind which comes from eating fruit) keeps us from seeing how close God really is.

Let's end with Moses. When Moses experiences the call to lead his people from slavery, he asks God for his name. The name which God gives is "Yahweh," which means in Hebrew "I am who I am." In other words, when Moses asks God for his name, God answers that he doesn't have a name; he is nameless. Moses wishes to pin God down by naming him. God doesn't allow that to happen. With words we can only come to a partial picture of God. God is best experienced not in the head, but in the heart.

Chapter Two
SIN AND THE AFTERLIFE

SIN has always been a big thing in the Catholic Church. It's been a big thing in all the Christian denominations. From many of the sermons which used to be preached (and still are in some places), one would think the main reason God made us was so we could feel guilty. I remember as a child wishing I had died before reaching the age of seven. Then I would have gone straight to heaven. After seven, it was almost impossible. At seven, I, along with everyone else, reached the "age of reason." I could determine what was right and what was wrong. I was, therefore, liable for judgment. I would need to keep track of my sins and make sure they were confessed. Otherwise, I would be spending a very long time in a place called purgatory or an even longer time in a place called hell. At seven, I knew I was in trouble.

One of the primary religious messages I was given as a child was that I was a sinner. I was walking a tightrope. The whole world was marked with a "danger" sign. I even needed to be on guard against the thoughts that bubbled up within me. I was to be ever vigilant. If I made just one slip, the devil would pounce on me with a vengeance. Being human was a real scary condition. The Good News sounded more like Bad News.

As a child I used to go to confession almost every week. If I missed my weekly confession, I would

begin to feel a despairing sense of guilt. I was afraid
the devil would try to arrange an accident if I had too
many unconfessed sins. The sisters in school had
told us how tricky the devil could be. They would tell
us the story of a sinner who built his house next door
to the rectory. That way when it came time for him to
die, he could get the priest over in a hurry. The sinner, of course, always died on vacation. I didn't want
to take any chances so I kept going to confession.
Sometimes I couldn't even think of much to say. Of
course, I was always guilty of fighting with my twin
brother and disobeying my mother. Those were my
two standards.

Just one sin could make you spend eternity in hell.
If you had an impure thought for too long, you could
be heading for hell. If you kissed your girl friend too
passionately, you had better head for confession. If
you stole a dollar or more, hell was probable; under a
dollar was a venial sin. A venial sin bought you time
in purgatory. A mortal sin gave you a ticket to hell. I
remember, at age ten, thinking I had committed a
mortal sin. I had seen a movie in which the word
"damn" was used. I was convinced I had seen one of
those "dirty" movies that the priest was always
preaching about. I still remember the feeling of relief
when I had confessed. I also remember the fear I felt
beforehand.

Such views of sin weren't very healthy. Yet many
of us are still suffering the consequences of these
views. We became ensnared at such an early age that
we couldn't really fight back. We wound up in a
prison and many of us still haven't found the key. We

might feel anger about what we were taught, but we're not sure what to do about it. It's not that we shouldn't have a sense of sin. Society would be difficult without an awareness of sin. People who feel no guilt, who have no conscience, are spoken of as "sociopathic personalities." A healthy notion of sin helps to integrate us. It helps us realize our human potential. But a healthy notion of sin is a rare thing. Let's take a look at some possible reasons why this is so.

When we were young Catholics, preparing for our first confession, we were taught the Act of Contrition. This was something we said at the end of confession to let God know we were really sorry for our sins. It went something like this: "O, my God, I am heartily sorry for having offended you, who are all-good and deserving of praise. I firmly resolve, with the help of your grace, never more to offend you, to do my penance, and to amend my life. Amen." Most people who go to confession today still say something along these lines at the end of their confession. (Note: Confession is now spoken of as the Sacrament of Reconciliation. I believe this new terminology speaks of a better theology. Yet, for the sake of clarity, I will continue to use the term with which most of us are familiar.)

The problem with the act of contrition is the notion of sin being an "offense" against God. It implies that God can be hurt by our sins. It makes God dependent on us. If there's a lot of sinning on a particular day, then God will be upset. If there are fewer sins than normal, then God will be happy. It puts God within our control. It's up to us to determine what kind of day he's going to have. But God, of course, is not in our control. God is not "offended" by what we may or may not do.

Besides implying that God is in our control, the idea of "offending" also implies a response. If God is hurt by what we do, he will naturally respond in some way. Even children understand this. They know if they do something wrong and get caught, they will have to pay some consequence. If God is hurt by what we do, then there must be some punishment coming. It might be dangled over our head for the future. God can certainly "get even" with the weapons of purgatory and hell. And when we offend someone, they will usually get angry. Someone who is angry must be appeased. So we return to the Old Testament God who gets angry and is always ready to destroy. His wrath must be turned aside with sacrifices and rituals. God is seen as having a short fuse.

Some preachers like to have a God with a short fuse. They claim that since our age is such a sinful age (every age has been proclaimed as more sinful than the age preceding it), God is going to get even. He's going to wipe everything out. This time he'll use nuclear weapons instead of a flood. God will release his pent-up hostility with nuclear annihilation. I've heard such a sermon. Yet what kind of God would this be and why would anyone want to worship him?

The simple truth is that God is neither offended nor angered by our sins. Knowing the human heart as he does, sin comes as no surprise. God just keeps loving us, regardless what sins we commit. That's the central Christian message: God loves us no matter what. We can never get any more of God's love than we already have. We can never get any less. God's love does not decrease or increase depending upon our sinfulness. God's nature is to love us.

The problem with sin is that it can keep us from experiencing all the love which God has for us. It doesn't change the love. It just makes us less certain of it. Sin fractures us. But God is experienced as the opposite of fracturing. Sin breaks us. God binds us up. Sin destroys our essential unity. God makes us whole. The more sin there is in our lives, the more difficult it is to experience wholeness. But it doesn't mean that God is withholding his love or healing. Sin doesn't make us enemies of God.

It's difficult at times to get this idea of God's never-ending, never-changing love across to people. We weren't raised to believe in this kind of love. I don't remember ever being told that God would love me no matter what I did. Yet isn't that the Good News? God's love has no strings attached. It doesn't depend on me. God loves the greatest saint and the greatest sinner the same. Many of us don't think that's fair. Yet look at Jesus' parable about the workers in the vineyard. Some work all day, some half a day, some just an hour. Yet all receive the same pay. God is like that. All his children are loved equally.

Some of us might even believe that God loves the sinner more than the saint. I was preaching one Sunday and I asked the question: "Who does God love more—the saint or the sinner?" What I was leading to was the message that God loves both the same. I asked people to raise their hands in favor of the saint or sinner. Many more people raised their hands for the sinner. They believed God would love the sinner more than the saint. If that were true, the logical conclusion would be we should sin as much as we can because then God would love us more.

Let's take a look at what happens in confession. I've spent a lot of time hearing people's confessions. For three years, I was a confessor at St. Peter's Church in downtown Chicago, one of the nation's busiest churches. Confessions were heard from six in the morning until eight at night. I heard thousands of confessions while working there. Being on the listening end of confessions helps one to hear how people approach sin.

To be a good confessor requires a certain personality or, at least, lots of grace. I'm afraid I'm not a very good confessor. I get angry fairly often while listening to what people confess. I'm not angry all the time, but often enough to help me see that being a confessor is not a strong point in my ministry. I get upset when people come to confession and tell me that it's been a year or longer since their last confession but they don't have any sins to confess. They might tell me that they are "too old to sin," as if sinning is reserved for the young. I get upset with people who would come to confession every day because of a twisted sense of guilt. I get upset with the needless suffering that some people endure because of how they were taught about sin. Much of what goes on in confession doesn't strike me as very healthy.

The sacrament surely has a purpose, but there are times when I wonder.

What about the person who finds no sin within themselves after a year? What are they looking for and where are they looking? What about the persons who claim they are too old to sin? The problem here stems from being taught that sin is especially sexual sin. Sexual sins were the "biggies" on the mortal sin rolls. It seemed we could get to hell quicker with sex than any other way. And while sexuality is certainly an arena with potential sins, it should never be the only or primary focus in our search for sinfulness. The church often lead us to believe that salvation would primarily be a sexual battle.

We can easily admit that the church hasn't dealt very well with sex. Perhaps that's to be expected when you have an all-celibate male leadership. Yet, regardless of the cause, the church's over-concern with sexual sins has caused untold suffering. For instance, what do you say to an eighty-year-old woman who's afraid to die because she has sexual thoughts? I'd like to take her hand and say, "Good for you, honey!" I'm delighted to know we don't lose our desire with the passage of time. Yet how can this woman have an easy death when it comes time for her? She lives in dread of judgment. Maybe she dwells too long on an old memory. Maybe she remembers the joys she once found in her husband's arms. What kind of God would condemn her for such thoughts? And, yet, isn't that what she was taught to believe? Weren't many of us taught the same way?

Part of the problem is that when we were taught about mortal sins, we were given a shortened lesson. When we were told something was a mortal sin, we should have been reminded that it had to fulfill the requirements for mortal sin. It had to completely cut us off from God and we had to want such a separation. Mortal sins are very rare birds. They are possible, but unusual. They are not nearly as common as we were led to believe. As long as we are honestly struggling to grow, we needn't be too concerned with the notion of mortal sin. Sin is real, but sin which makes us inaccessible to God's love is mostly unreal.

One of the things I hear confessed most often is masturbation. I've always wanted to preach a sermon on masturbation. I never have. It would be difficult to do with younger children in the audience. I'm also afraid of the possible reaction. Masturbation seems such a big sin to so many Catholics. Often I will ask the person confessing masturbation whether they consider it a mortal sin. Almost everyone says yes. Every once in a while, someone will say they aren't sure.

I will sometimes try to talk with the person confessing masturbation. I will say that while masturbation is something which might cut us off from God, it would be incredibly unlikely. If the person confessing is male, I will also mention how part of the church's concern with masturbation stemmed from a faulty understanding of human reproduction. Up to a hundred years ago, the sperm was thought to contain the complete child. The woman was seen as being an incubator for the child. It's no wonder, then, that the church considered masturbation to be so wrong. It was seen as the destruction of a complete child, akin to abortion. The church never did discuss female masturbation very much. They probably considered it unlikely.

When I try to take away some of the guilt from masturbation, people will sometimes fight me. There are some who will question whether I am a valid priest. There are some who write to higher ecclesiastical authorities. It seems some people need the guilt they feel. They hold tenaciously to it if I try to take it away. Maybe guilt glues some people together. Maybe it serves a purpose. I'm not sure of the answer. But what bothers me is the kind of life possible for someone held together by guilt.

Some people, of course, are thankful for what I say. They will tell me they have never heard that masturbation is not as sinful as they were taught. That surprises me. It surprises me because I know many priests and most of them hold similar views as mine concerning masturbation. Few priests I know consider it a significant sin. Maybe priests find it difficult to keep bringing the issue up to people who come to confess. Maybe it's more prudent to let people alone. Maybe a person's awareness of sin is too delicate to tamper with. Those are possibilities. Yet I still believe that misplaced guilt is a poison. A sense of sin is not the same thing as fear of punishment.

Guilt and a sense of sin are related but they're not the same thing. I'd like to quote Thomas Merton, a Trappist monk who died in 1968: "Guilt is a sense of oppression from the outside: an experience of anxiety in which one feels that he's going to be called to account for a misdeed. Sin is a sense of evil within myself, not because I have violated a law outside myself but because I have violated the inmost laws of my own being, which are, at the same time, the laws of God who dwells in me." We feel guilt when we expect punishment from those who hold power over us. Too often churches have produced lots of guilt with little sense of sin. We avoided sin because we were afraid of hell, not because sin was an internal untruth. And because of guilt, we distorted our vision of God.

Let's look again at the eighty-year-old woman with sexual thoughts. She's afraid of being punished. Yet sexual thoughts can hardly be controlled. The more we try to suppress our thoughts and feelings, the more they demand attention. Sexual imaginings are part of our make-up. They aren't attacks from outside of us. They are part of us. We can't do battle against them unless we do battle against ourselves. And many of us were taught to do such battle. Instead of just accepting our sexuality, we were made to feel it was something foreign to us. Our passions were the work of Satan, rather than being part of our humanity. We do need to discipline ourselves. We don't need to go to war.

As Drs. Terruwe and Baars note in *Psychic Wholeness and Healing:* "When a person represses feelings of a sexual nature because he thinks they are sinful or too sensual, he logically proceeds to repress all sensual feelings." We begin to have a Puritan sense of life, devoid of many human pleasures. Look at the

Christian denominations which still forbid something like dancing. How could God not wish us to dance? What kind of crippled people do we harvest when we make them fearful of feelings and passions?

Yet how often have we thought of the saintly person as one who looks dour, as if they lived on lemons? Look at the somber colors we've made our religious wear. My lovely Irish mother has been after me for over ten years to buy a black suit. But I have refused. I do not want to wear either a black suit or a Roman collar. Neither, to me, is a good sign for the God whom I serve. And while there is something to be said for being recognized as a priest, it can also lead to the "clericalism" that has "bedeviled" the church. I find it adequate to wear my brown Franciscan habit when there is a need for "religious" garb. I also realize that decisions about what I wear are my decisions. Somber colors have a place. Bright colors also have a place. To wear somber colors all the time would probably make me somber. There are enough somber people already.

The colors with which we try to wrap our ecclesiastics speak about our sense of life and our sense of sin. Either we fear life or we don't. Unfortunately, our religion has often made us fear life. If we try, for instance, to suppress our sexuality, must we not also suppress our pleasure at being alive? Are spirituality and sexuality opposites? As theologian Michael Novak notes: "For many persons it is only, or chiefly, in sexual love that one encounters the category of an end in itself, the category of the sacred. It is from this experience, for many, that religious language becomes meaningful again." Sexuality and spirituality are not opposites. Both have to do with becoming open. If we close off parts of ourselves, then we will miss out on becoming whole. Not that we are free to do whatever we desire. Yet openness is our quest.

Many of us were raised to follow rules instead of developing our own values. We learned how long we could safely kiss someone, as if God carried a stopwatch. The more rules we were given, the less we had to struggle with our own lives. But if all our moral values come from the outside, then we have given up control of ourselves. And that's exactly what many of us did in the past and, in some ways, still do. We were given a catalogue of what could and couldn't be done. All we had to do was follow the "game plan" and we would lessen our chances of hellfire. Naturally, our freedom would also be lessened and, along with it, our ability to love.

The church became like a parent who, when asked by their child why they had to do something, gives the answer, "Because I said so!" Our moral code was tied to our acceptance of the church. If we believed in the absolute integrity of the church, then we found it rather easy to follow the rules. Even if we came to appreciate the humanity of the church, we still were tied to a system of rules. The church viewed her members as children who must be continually helped in their moral decisions. Most of us went along because we didn't have many options. If the church held the key to salvation, then we would have to play by her rules. Of course, by going along we would remain children.

Even today, I still get calls from grown men and women who ask me if it's all right for them to do something. It might be wanting to go to communion without an hour's fast. They want my permission and then everything will be all right. But it won't be all right. We need to make our own moral decisions, even though we will make some wrong decisions. It's the only way we can discover our own internal moral compass, our conscience. We must work to fashion our conscience and to heed its voice. Neither will happen if the church shouts out what we should do. Our inner voice will be overwhelmed.

The church, like all mothers, doesn't want her children to get hurt. One of the ways to make life less dangerous is to have many rules and regulations laid out in a guidebook. Then when you feel lost, you turn to the guidebook and find the solution. Guidebooks serve a purpose. But the church tried to have an answer for every question that might be encountered. That way people would be protected, or so it was thought. The church's intentions may have been laudable but there were mixed results. By keeping us "safe," the church was also keeping us from learning how to live in the world. The world was portrayed as being black and white: right and wrong. We weren't taught how to deal with the enormous grey areas of life. The "guidebook wasn't meant to handle grey, and by trying to follow it we became eternal children.

The reason most of us were willing to keep following a rulebook was our fear of hell. We avoided sin primarily because it could send us to hell. So let's take a look at hell. Where did the idea come from? Is hell acceptable in a healthy religion?

Through most of the Old Testament times there was no heaven and hell. Once you were dead, you stayed dead. You would go to *Sheol*, but there was no awareness. Death was an end. There could be no system of reward and punishment except in this life. The only way God could show his favor was while you were still living. Therefore, long life, many possessions, and many children were seen by the Israelites as being signs of God's favor. If you died young; if you were poor; if you had no children, then it was likely you were being punished for your sins (or the sins of your ancestors or your king). It was a simple theology. It just didn't work out in practice. Many who were good suffered while those who were evil prospered.

The Old Testament Book of Job tried to wrestle with this problem. Job endures all kinds of misfortunes. His many possessions are destroyed. His children are killed. His body becomes covered with sores. And he doesn't understand why all these things have happened. He demands to bring his case before God. His friends come and insist that he is only being punished for his sins or the sins of his ancestors. But Job insists on his innocence. One of his visitors suggests the possibility of an afterlife where everything will balance, but Job rejects the idea. He keeps insisting on speaking to God. Finally, God does speak to Job. God asks Job some pointed questions about how the world is run. It is not Job who is in charge of things. God is God and that's that.

God's ways are not man's ways. So Job asks forgiveness for his complaints. And, in a passage added on to the original story, Job gets new possessions, new children, and his sufferings come to an end.

The story of Job gives us a partial answer. It shows that the Old Testament writers were struggling to understand. As this struggle continued through Old Testament times, the idea of an afterlife became more and more acceptable. By the time of Jesus, there were many who believed you would continue after death. Along with this belief came the ideas of heaven and hell. If one didn't pay for their sins in this life, they would have to pay in the next. If you were good, you would be rewarded with heaven.

The people who lived near the Israelites no doubt had an influence in the development of afterlife concepts. The Egyptians held to an afterlife, but only if your body continued. That belief led to their embalming practices. They also believed your soul would be weighed on the scales of judgment. If you failed the test, you would be given over to Ammut, the eater of the dead; part crocodile, part hippopotamus, part lion. Persian mythology had something similar. Rashnu was in charge of the scales. If you passed, you went to a place of joy and pleasure. If you failed, you went to a place of pain and punishment. Through contact with these people and others, the theology of the Israelites became diffused with diverse religious ideas. The Persian notions of heaven and hell were taken by some Israelites to be likely solutions to the questions raised in Job.

The word used by the Israelites for hell was *Ge-*

henna, which was a garbage dump outside of Jerusalem. It burned day and night. So, if you were evil in this life, you would wind up in *Gehenna.* That's the word which Jesus also used. From *Gehenna* came our Christian idea of hell. It was a place of fire where you would burn forever. It was ruled over by Satan, just as Hades ruled the underworld in Greek mythology. Hell became a cornerstone of Christian theology. It was preached in ways that gave many sleepless nights. Writers, like Dante, poured forth descriptions of the horrors of hell. Hell became part of our heritage.

All of us who are Catholics were raised with the idea of hell. It was impossible to avoid hearing about it. I was acutely aware of hell as a child. Whenever I would burn my finger or get sunburned at the beach, I would be reminded of hell. I prayed I would be lucky enough to make it to purgatory. Purgatory was a place like hell, but it didn't last forever. Most of us figured we could never get straight to heaven. And while we don't hear very much about hell these days, it still seems to lurk in the shadows, like a mugger or rapist.

I am not sure what I believe any longer about hell or purgatory. I'm sure that I don't see them the same way I did as a child. I don't see them as places of punishment. I see purgatory as a process that most, if not all, of us will have to undergo upon dying. It's like going outside on a very sunny day. The bright sunlight can hurt our eyes if we have been in the dark. If God is seen as a great light, then we will have to endure some adjustment as we come to him. I see purgatory, therefore, as a process; not as a place where we "serve time."

If purgatory isn't a place, how does that change things? There are some of us who have masses said for those who have died. The belief is that God will shorten their "sentence" if masses are offered. I'm not at all sure what good is accomplished by having masses said for the deceased. I've run into a bit of trouble because of my doubt. One day after mass in Parma, Ohio, a woman asked me if I believed in purgatory. I said that I didn't believe in it as a place. She told me that she was attending that mass because it was being offered for her recently deceased husband. I tried to explain my doubt, but I don't think I did a very good job.

I felt some internal hypocrisy because of the woman's question. Every mass that is celebrated has an intention behind it. Someone will offer a few dollars to have someone remembered in a special way at mass. Now I can't see a God who would pluck people out of purgatory because they've had so many masses offered for them. Yet mass offerings are still a healthy addition to priests' salaries, including my own. To be honest about this, I should not accept money for masses remembering those who are deceased. I am not always as honest as I could be.

It was shortly after speaking with this woman in Parma that I received a phone call. The first thing the caller did was ask me if I believed in purgatory. I knew I was in trouble again. The caller identified himself as one of the local pastors. He demanded to know how I could consider myself a Catholic priest and not believe in purgatory. I tried to explain. He ended the conversation by telling me that he would have to bring the matter to the attention of the bishop in Cleveland. I didn't hear any more about it, but I did realize the care that is needed when it comes to discussing the afterlife.

Let's get back to the idea of hell. I'm not sure what to believe anymore. I certainly don't see hell in terms of fire. I don't see it as a place of torture. I'm not even sure if I believe in hell at all. I think I have trouble with the word itself. I would like to totally dismiss the word from normal usage. The word itself needs to be purged. It has too many destructive connotations attached to it. Yet I'm not too sure that I would want to get rid of the concept altogether. In one sense I agree with what William Silverman says in *God Help Me!*: "The concept of hell has no place in a liberal, mature religious faith. It is inconsistent with reason and constitutes an unspeakable blasphemy against God. A heavenly Father who damns is not worthy of the love of his children. To exploit God as a theological bogeyman to frighten the ignorant and the naive is inimical to the belief in a God of love." Yet, in another sense, I have come to see the need for the concept of hell.

Reading *What Are They Saying about the End of the World?* by one of my former teachers, Zachary Hayes, helped me hold on to at least a skepticism regarding hell. If we are free, then there must be the possibility of rejecting God, not only here but forever. Hell is not a place then, but a "state of heart." The person has freely chosen to be closed to love. Now to admit such a possibility doesn't mean that anyone is in hell. The church has never stated there is anyone in hell. But the concept does seem necessary if we are truly free. If everyone is saved, regardless of whether they want to be, then where is our freedom? I can't imagine how or why anyone would close themselves off from God. Yet if the possibility doesn't exist, then I am not free and, subsequently, not human.

So I'm in a kind of "limbo" regarding hell. I guess I really do believe that God will take care of all his children. I don't know how that will work out in practice. I guess I don't need to know. I guess that I'm also reacting to many of the things I was taught as a child. Many of us, for instance, were taught you had to be a Christian to get to heaven. Catholics came very close to being taught you couldn't get to heaven unless you were a Catholic. But either of these beliefs dismisses the majority of people living on our world. There are over four billion people alive. Only one billion of them are even nominally Christian. What do we do with the other three billion people? Where do they go when they die? The notion of limbo as a place where unbaptized go has been dropped as a theological concept. Certainly we can't throw them all into hell, even if it does exist. Somehow God must take care of them. They are also his children.

Look at the ways we used hell against people. We were taught such things that if you ate meat on Friday, you could go to hell. Yet what kind of God would be concerned with what we ate or when? The Israelites had many laws concerning what could or couldn't be eaten. Many of their laws made sense in light of the health risks involved in eating certain foods. The difficulty arises when such rules are claimed to come from God. Such a claim distorts our idea of God.

Hell was used to threaten people. Yet healthy people don't need threats to make them behave. But there is a fear of hell within me that runs very deep. I hope our children can grow up without such fears making a home in them. The world is a difficult enough place without having to deal with threats of eternal damnation.

The notion of hell, as commonly taught, appeals to the self-righteous among us. We want God to condemn those who don't live as we expect them to live. We damn those who have different lifestyles than our own. We want God to take care of our enemies. We want a place of eternal punishment. It helps us assume that we're better than our neighbors. We go to church. They don't. We're going to heaven. They're going to hell. We can go through life dividing people into those "saved" and those "damned." Hell makes a handy weapon. Hell is very often a prison invented by our own hearts where we can throw those who displease us. The tragedy is that we don't realize that hell is a place fashioned by human hands. We lay the blame on God.

Look at what Jonathan Edwards, an early American preacher, had to say. He claimed those in heaven would be able to see the tortures of those in hell. Because of this, those saved will love God all the more. But such an idea is revolting. Are we supposed to watch people in agony and delight in it? Such an idea can only come from a sadistic psyche. Yet aren't we all a bit twisted when we look for someplace to banish those we either fear or hate?

Jesus used the concept of hell when he was with us. Yet that doesn't, in itself, make it real. When Jesus took on our humanity, he took on our ignorance. With incarnation Jesus accepted the extent of human knowledge available at that time. He didn't know the world was round. He didn't know about nuclear physics. He grew in his knowledge, limited by what was then known. This is tricky ground. Jesus was truly God and truly man. But just as he spoke Aramaic, so he spoke in the religious terminology of his time. If Jesus was reincarnated in our country today, he would speak English and use our contemporary religious concepts. Jesus certainly broadened the religious understanding of his time. He expressed religious truths which continue to startle us with their simple profundity. Yet these truths were couched in the images of his time. Jesus used the notion of hell as a place of punishment. I don't think he would continue to use such an image if he were born today.

I have yet to use the word hell in a sermon. I'm just not sure what to do with it. The word conveys much more than it should. So I avoid the problem by avoiding the word. That's what one would call an intellectual or moral cop-out, yet I'm not sure what other path to take. I don't want to see our freedom jeopardized by denying hell's possibility. But I also don't want to have people living and dying in fear. Hell should stay in hell.

What about heaven? Most of us were taught to

picture heaven as being above us somewhere. If we got to heaven, we would sit on a cloud and play a harp. But I don't want to spend eternity sitting on some cloud, playing some lousy harp. Heaven really wasn't pictured as being very attractive. Most of us weren't excited about the prospects of heaven. We were more concerned with avoiding hellfire.

Heaven means being fully with God. Most of us will have to die to experience such communion. I don't believe that heaven will be passive; certainly not cloud-sitting or harp-playing. I think we'll be able to somehow be with those who have died before us. I look forward to meeting my father again, along with the grandparents I never met. I don't believe that our spirits are recycled, like those who believe in reincarnation. We are all special with an individuality that will not die. I don't know much beyond that. I do know that God will take care of me when I die. That's all I need to know. Maybe heaven, like hell, is a "state of heart." Like the drop of rain falling into the ocean, I look forward to "falling into" God.

Chapter Three
MORE SIN STUFF

WHAT is sin anyway? What should we confess if and when we go to confession? Certainly we would be foolish to confess our sexual feelings. But accepting our feelings doesn't mean we can always act on them. It's the same with anger. Many people confess they "got angry." But is anger a sin? It's a natural reaction to being hurt. It's a part of our biological make-up. If we don't get angry when we are hurt, then we can be sure there's something wrong with us. The Gospels clearly portray Jesus as getting angry. The sin is not with the reaction of anger. Sin lies with what we do with anger. If we throw a temper tantrum, if we injure someone physically or psychologically, then the question of sin arises. Sin arises when we hurt ourselves or others. There is a malicious element involved.

Actually, it could be sinful not to get angry. If anger is denied, it gets turned against ourselves. It is free, then, to do all kinds of damage. There are also times when we should feel anger. When we see injustice, when we see bigotry, when we see useless destruction, we should respond with anger. As Matthew Fox notes in *On Becoming a Musical Mystical Bear*: "When one's capacity to become outraged at injustices is smothered and barely smolders, so does one's capacity for loving justice. Anger is as sure a signal of love as smoke is of fire."

I remember the anger I felt while at places like the Berlin Wall and the concentration camp at Dachau. If I had not felt anger and outrage, I could be sure of something missing inside of me. Anger is not a sin. It's an essential and healthy emotion. If we were taught to deny it or suppress it, we were taught wrong. What we do with anger is the concern, not whether we feel it. Of course, many of us may see the world in such a way that we get angry much too easily. If we are constantly being annoyed and upset, we would be well advised to do some soul-searching.

What about other sins? What about the sin of prejudice? I've heard thousands of confessions. Yet in all those confessions, I've only heard two or three people confess the sin of prejudice or racism. We just weren't taught to see it as sinful. We weren't usually taught about the social dimension of sin. Sin was something personal, between God and me. Social sins weren't spoken of very much.

Sin has to do with certain sensitivities. The more we develop our humanity, the more aware we become of sin. We see the ways we turn away from love. We see the ways we bring destruction to our world. We accept our responsibility for global sins. With such sensitivities, we try to be more caring and careful. We try to avoid sin because when we don't we feel pain within our hearts and souls.

The closer we get to God, the more we see our own sinfulness and the more we want to deal with it. The more sensitive we become to sin, the more we want to keep it from our lives. This sensitivity has to do with opening our hearts. It's not a crippling sense of guilt. It's an ability to see deeper and farther.

Take, for example, the wildlife destruction that has been part of our history. Isn't such destruction sinful? Yet it doesn't get preached much. What about buying fur coats, especially from endangered species? We need to be more aware of what we're doing. If we kill something, there should be a reason, a need. All living things are our brothers and sisters. One doesn't need to be fanatical. If a mosquito attacks me, I will slap it. If a fly buzzes around my food, I will try to kill it. But the point is to be aware of the killing. Is it necessary? Does it serve some purpose? Can it be avoided without great loss? I used to have ants come into my office when I lived in Parma, Ohio. I would pick them up and return them outside. It's not that I care much about ants. It's just I saw no reason to kill them.

But just because I was unwilling to kill those ants doesn't mean I have my sensitivities straight. I can still be vindictive and cruel. Sometimes I am more careful with animal life than with the lives of those around me. But perhaps by becoming more sensitive to life in general, I will become especially sensitive to human life. It's all part of an educational process. Learning more and more helps us to see more and more. Not that learning by itself makes us sensitive. But the more I can learn about the world in which I live, the more aware I am about what I am doing in the world. I will be able to see connections. I will understand sin in a broader way than previously. I will see how life is joined together, and I will want to treat all life with respect.

Maybe we focused primarily on sexual sins in the past because then we didn't have to deal with sins having a broad scope. We could ignore the broad questions. We didn't have to wrestle with the violence which is so much a part of our American society. We didn't have to be much concerned with how we treated the Indians, the blacks, and many of the other ethnic groups who came to our shores. We didn't have to be troubled with the abuses of power which were (and are) part and parcel of business. The ways we dehumanized those around us could be ignored.

As long as we were struggling with sexuality, we could feel satisfied that we were battling our sinfulness. Sexuality was the prime target. Our pettiness and prejudices could come later. We developed a certain near-sightedness, a moral myopia, which would make possible the self-righteousness so prevalent among church-goers. It would also make possible priests who abused their parishioners with their sermons, imagining that because of their celibacy they were less sinful than the rest of humanity.

We were taught that sins were things we *did*. The emphasis was on the doing. Sin had an active element to it. But we never learned about sin's passive side. We also sin by *not* doing. When we don't care, when we neglect opportunities for loving behavior, when we allow injustice to go unchallenged, when we refuse to consider other points of view, we sin. We often neglect this side of sin when we examine ourselves. We just weren't taught to look at sin's underside. It was like exercising only half the body.

Let's look at some other possible areas of sin. What about when we try to impose our will on others? What about parents who try to fashion their children to meet parental expectations? What about priests who lord it over their parishioners? What about religious superiors who presume to know the will of God for those under their care? What about the ways we pollute and abuse our environment? What about the ways we contribute to violence, including the verbal kind?

Take the issue of handguns. The proliferation of handguns has been termed a national disgrace. Yet how often do we hear about it in sermons? It can certainly be a volatile subject. I preached on handguns once in Quincy, Illinois. The Mississippi Valley Gun Club quickly demanded equal time. I find myself unwilling to enter a house where there are guns. Once I was taking the weekend schedule of masses and confessions for a pastor who was away on vacation. The church was somewhere in southern Indiana. In the bedroom of the rectory was an assortment of rifles. I found myself unable to sleep in the rectory.

But just because I see guns as evil, doesn't mean others should see them the same way. Everybody shouldn't see everything the same. Yet we need to develop sensitivities. It would be sinful for me to own a handgun. For someone else it might be a necessity. I can't extrapolate from myself and claim it's a sin for everyone to own a handgun. I can only raise the reasons why it would be sinful for me. We need to share our sensitivities. By sharing what we see, we can all grow morally. And to grow morally is to grow in healthy religion. How we view sin has a real impact on how we view God.

Let's examine where sin and evil come from. I was taught that sin and evil had a lot to do with the devil. I don't remember exactly how the story was presented, but it had something to do with a test. I was always being tested to see if I was "strong" or not. The devil would keep presenting me with opportunities for sin and would delight if I "fell."

Most of us heard a lot about the devil during our Catholic upbringing. He seemed to be more present to us than God himself. The devil had at his command a whole horde of other devils. I think we were "assigned" a personal devil, just as we had a guardian angel: all the makings of a cosmic battle. The bad angels fought the good angels. The war zone was the earth and we were the booty.

The idea of the devil as a "tester" or "tempter" comes from the Book of Job. Satan is upset because God is always boasting about how good Job is. Satan claims that Job's faith and goodness result from all the good things Job has, so God allows everything to be eventually taken away. Satan keeps pressing until there is nothing left but Job wins the test. He gets everything back in the end.

Satan in this story is not an enemy of God. It is only in later literature that he becomes an enemy instead of the one who tests. He becomes the one who rebelled and lost. Such a notion of Satan helps explain many things. But what happens is evil gets removed from its real source in the human heart and becomes a distinct personality.

Now I certainly believe in evil. I also believe it can be spoken of in a personal way. But I don't believe in the conceptualization of evil known as Satan. Evil may have its own existence in some way. Perhaps it's some kind of spiritual force growing from the evil we find within ourselves. Yet it's very difficult to divide the world into good and evil. The world is a mixture of each, and it's doubtful one can be separated from the other. By presupposing a devil, the problem of good and evil is transferred from us. It becomes something "out there" rather than something existing within our own hearts.

There is evil, of course, which has no human element, such as earthquakes, tidal waves, storms, and the like. But environmental evil has no maliciousness behind it. It just is. It's part of the world and must be accepted as a condition for living in the world. The evil I'm talking about has a direction behind it. It's what is known as sin. It comes from the human heart. And if its origin is denied, then it can never be dealt with. If it's seen as arising from Satan, then we can always claim "the Devil made me do it." But we need to look for sin's origin within ourselves, rather than hunting creatures having horns and tails.

Another problem with the existence of Satan is why would God have created him in the first place? If God knows the future, as most theologians argue, then why would he have given life to Satan, knowing what would happen? Knowing all the evil which would be unleashed upon creation, why would God have brought him into existence? Some suggest that while God knows all there is to know, the future cannot be known and is, therefore, unknowable even to God. Some propose we need Satan as "the tester." Yet if God put us here on earth to play some kind of game, then something is not quite right. Why would God give us life just to play a game? Wouldn't God already know the results, since he knows the future? He would know which of us would pass and which would fail. Why bother with the game at all? It's not much of a reason for our being given life. Yet there are many religious people who hold such a view. It's still one possible answer for why we're here, but I have difficulties with such a solution. God would not be very far removed from the capricious antics of the gods and goddesses of Mount Olympus.

We must be especially careful with children. If we bring up the idea of Satan to them, they will have a hard time understanding what he's supposed to symbolize. Children should not be exposed to the notion of Satan unless they are first taught that Satan is not real. Maybe it's time to attempt a new symbolization for the reality of evil. Satan, as symbol, has outlived most of his usefulness.

If there is no Satan, where did evil come from? If God is all good, how did we wind up so flawed? The story of Adam and Eve puts the blame on the snake and on the woman. The Greeks put the blame on Pandora and her box. But should we keep looking for someone to blame? Was the world at any time a paradise? It wouldn't seem so. The world seems to have always been a place of struggle, a place of violence, a place of pain. The arrival of humans added the dimension of sin. Sin has a rebelliousness inherent in it, a willfulness. There may have been an innocence before humanity's arrival but the innocence was of an instinctual kind. When the first humans came out of the evolutionary mist, the instinctual innocence was broken.

So the story of Adam and Eve does have a certain truth to it. Humans may have shattered some form of existing innocence. That's not to say the innocence shouldn't have been shattered. Life gained an understanding of itself within humanity's mind. And with this understanding came a new form of evil. We haven't yet come to terms with it. We have spent much of our history searching for someone or something to blame. We break the mirrors which have been held up for us. We prefer to avoid them because they point the finger of blame back at us.

God, in giving us life, also gave us freedom. Without that freedom, we would not be able to love. Love must be free or else it doesn't exist. God gave us life so we might become true lovers. Freedom was essential. But the price of that freedom was sin. Being free and being sinful seem to be connected. God gave up control over us in order that we might learn how to love. We are, in some ways, on our own: not abandoned but, rather, set free. God's spirit is always with us, pushing us on towards love. Either we allow ourselves to get swept up in that spirit, or else we shun it and walk stubborn-faced against it. The more we walk against it, the more sin enters our lives. Yet there must be that possibility. We must be able to

freely choose to love. We must also be able to freely
choose to sin. Our greatest problem, sin, is but the
reverse side to our greatest gift: love.

How do we deal with our sinfulness? One of the
things we must do first is accept the fact of our
brokenness. We must acknowledge our dark side,
sometimes spoken of as "the shadow." If we refuse
to see the darkness of our own hearts, then we cannot have any control over it. If we don't admit its
existence, then it's free to do whatever damage it
wants. We must accept ownership if we want any
hope of influencing it. And while I'm speaking of the
dark side as "it," I don't want to imply that it's distinct from who I am. It is part of me. If I don't acknowledge this part of me, then I am divided against
myself without even realizing it. By accepting our
divided heart, we have the possibility of making it
whole. If we refuse, then we live in division.

It's something like self-acceptance. We need to accept ourselves, flaws included. Otherwise, we will
keep thinking of ourselves as too short, too tall, too
fat, too skinny, too whatever. We focus on our flaws
and develop a body awareness that limps. It's the
same with our dark side. If we don't accept it, then
we go through life with a certain blindness, hurting
people because we don't see them. We stumble and
fall because we're not looking. We must first accept
our shadow and then learn the ways in which it
works. In such a way, we can throw light upon it. It
can be brought more and more into the arena of understanding.

I believe, generally speaking, in the need for the

sacrament of confession, of reconciliation. It can be a very healthy experience. It can also be an unhealthy one. Most of us keep going to confession in the same way, over and over. We confess the same sins, more or less, as we have always confessed. We are hesitant to look into the dark corners of our internal house. So we keep washing the same section of wall over and over. We need to broaden our work scope. Then we can begin to take more control over our internal home. The more we move around inside going from room to room, the more space there will be for God's spirit to work. The more we try to bring light to the dark corners, the less places there will be for creatures of the dark to hide. Healing will then happen. We will begin to become whole.

We need a time when we confront who we are. Without such times, we stumble through life and learn very little from all the things we trip over. Confession gives us an opportunity to see those things, to admit our mistakes and acknowledge the evil which has come from us. In confession we are also given a penance to perform. The penance shows we are sorry, while trying to strike a new balance. In the past, we were usually given "Our Father's and Hail Mary's" to say as a penance. Now many priests suggest other types of penances, more closely related to the sins confessed. In such a way, we see the obligation to counterbalance the evil which has been born into the world because of our sin.

A lot of things have been written about the ways Catholics were raised. Some of what has been written is funny and wise. Some is angry and resentful.

But we all need to accept how we were raised. The church was very much like a mother to us. And just as we must all eventually make peace with our parents if we want happiness, so we must achieve a certain peace with the church. Some of the things we were taught were not very healthy. Maybe we suffered a lot of guilt and fear. Yet I believe the church was trying to do her best. Just as many parents fall short of the mark when it comes to parenting, so the church has often fallen short when it comes to nurturing us. That doesn't absolve the church from the wrongs which were done, but it can help us live with the results.

It was the area of sin where many of us got stuck. Our children, however, will not be taught the same as we were. They will, hopefully, be taught that sin doesn't make God stop loving us. Yet there are a few who want the church to teach the same things she did in the past. They want the church to be a type of policeman. They want the Catholic schools to be places of strong discipline, as if the church's main role was to discipline children. But I don't think the church wants to retreat to the ways of the past.

And just as we struggle to understand what church means to us, so we continue to struggle with sin. The struggle with both only ends at the grave. What happens from the grave onward is in God's hands. Yet we can be sure that part of the human task is to make ourselves as lovable and as loving as possible. Sin is what keeps us from such a task.

We can have a healthy notion of sin, but it takes a great deal of effort. We don't need to throw out everything we were taught, but we must sift through it and discard what has lost its value. It's a bit like cleaning out the attic. We have to throw things out to make new space. Some of us have attics which are overcrowded. Some of us would rather not do any cleaning. We would prefer a church which tells us what to do and when. We would rather hold on to all the things we were taught, even if they are slowly strangling us. Some of us want to remain children. It seems safer.

The church of the past was often willing to keep us children. We weren't pushed out into adulthood when it was time. We were given the luxury of a ready-made puzzle, not having to put it together ourselves. But instead of helping us, this ready-made puzzle brought confusion to many. The answers didn't always fit the questions. Many became resentful and rebellious. A kind of wound opened up which has been difficult to treat, as if the old and new split away from each other. Many of us carry such a wound. We can all use some healing.

Chapter Four
PRAYER

THE ways we pray to God are good indicators of how we think about God. If we are always asking for things, then God becomes a kind of giant slot machine. The more prayers we put in, the more things we hope to get out. We pray for new houses, new jobs, new wives, new husbands, new children. And while it's all right to express the desires of our hearts, we should understand what such prayers imply about God. It's as if we're trying to strike some sort of deal with him "Okay, God, I'll pray these prayers if you do these things for me!" We suppose God will be anxious to go along because he somehow needs our prayers, like a junkie needs a fix. We can even try for bargains. But God does not need our prayers.

As a child, I prayed very often to God. I would ask for something and then promise not to fight with my twin brother for a whole week if I got what I wanted. I didn't get the things I asked for. It's probably just as well. I don't think I could have made it through a week without fighting. But I still kept wondering why I never got what I prayed for. Maybe I wasn't good enough. Maybe God didn't hear me. Even though I kept trying, I couldn't figure it out. I knew God was in charge. I just hoped he would like some advice from time to time.

It was especially difficult when it came time for my

father to die. He had been sick for a number of months with a brain tumor. There wasn't much hope for his recovery. I was eleven at the time. I believed if I prayed enough, then God would make my father get well. I prayed and prayed. Since I was also an altar boy, I figured that would help me get a hearing.

But my father didn't get better. He died and I was left in a great deal of confusion. Why would God let my father die, especially when I was praying so hard? There's a part of me that still doesn't understand. Part of the problem was the way I was taught about prayer. I was given the impression that if you prayed long and hard for something, then God would certainly do what you wanted. Well, I had prayed long and hard but nothing had happened. Something seemed to be wrong, either with God or with what I had been taught. At eleven, I wasn't sure what the answer was.

Years later I began to realize that prayer isn't intended to make God do what I want. I understood what Kierkegaard meant. Prayer doesn't change God. It changes the one who prays. Yet there are times when I would still like to tell God what he should be doing. I don't always understand the freedom which God has given me, a freedom which keeps God from directing my life as if I were a puppet on strings. My freedom, in a sense, limits what God can do and freedom is essential for love.

Since I am a priest, there are many times when people will ask me to say a prayer for their intentions. Some, I'm sure, believe that since I'm a priest, God will be more willing to hear my prayer than their prayer. People are often putting money into my hands and asking me to say a prayer for them or one of their relations. Do such prayers do any good? Yes, I think they do, but in a way different from what we were taught. Surely God doesn't take any more notice of my prayer than anyone else's. But by praying for someone, I show my concern and the concern of the church. It's this concern which is important. It's a form of embrace and we all need embraces, the physical and spiritual kind. Praying for someone is like hugging them. A good hug can do wonders.

Over the years, I've seen many of the ways prayer gets distorted. For example, just visit a church bingo game. If you look around when the game is in progress, you're more than likely to hear people praying to God. "C'mon, God, make this number B-6 and I'll give 50 percent of what I win to the church!" What image of God is being prayed to? Will God rig the game? Or visit Las Vegas and hear the prayers which get mumbled at the dice tables and roulette wheels.

Well, maybe such prayers don't seem to do any harm. But they do. They distort our image of God and make any relationship with him more difficult. Prayers should show our concern for each other, along with our desire for God. They shouldn't advocate greed and selfishness, which they often do. It's not that we shouldn't want good things for ourselves and those who are special to us. Self-love is an important part of any healthy religion.

But what do such prayers do to our image of God? Remember the television show, "The Millionaire," which was popular during the '50s? My family wasn't rich. In fact, we were poor. So I used to pray to God that the fellow from the "The Millionaire" would come to our house and give us a check for a million dollars, just as he did on the TV show. But he never came. And my image of God wavered.

Thinking God will do what we want if we keep asking long enough can keep many of us from taking life into our own hands. We keep praying to God to change something in our lives, instead of seeking our own solution. And if we don't get what we pray for then we assume things are the way they are meant to be. It must be God's will. We pray for health and if we don't get it, then we believe God wants us sick. We pray for God to change the dehumanizing marriage we're in and if he doesn't, then it must be his will.

We believe God is the cause of everything which happens. But is he? Does God control everything? I'm not sure. I mentioned earlier that the freedom which I have limits what God can do. This is a very difficult theological area. God seems to have given up control over certain things. By knowing the importance of freedom (without which love would be impossible), God gives us freedom over ourselves. Like a wise parent, God gives control over to his children. Otherwise, we would remain children forever. God gives us the freedom to discover who we are. Yet he also helps us on that journey of self-discovery. As Michael Novak says in *Belief and Unbelief*: "I take God to be the source of both the unrest and the rest of my spirit; the promoter of the drive to understand and its fulfillment."

When it comes to God, he is free and so are we. But we still keep trying to put God in chains. Look at all the superstitions which have been part of the church. As a child, I wore a brown scapular at all times. I was taught that if I died while wearing a scapular, I would get into heaven on the first Saturday after I died. That certainly seemed like a good deal, so I wore my scapular everywhere. I finally took it off, though, after hearing a story from one of the sisters who taught me. She told our class about this boy who lived a good life and wore a brown scapular (there were also green ones). But then the boy did something very wrong. We weren't told what. The boy got sick and started to die. But just before he died, the brown scapular began to burn into his chest. He tore off the scapular and then died. I took mine off not long afterwards. The game seemed rigged.

A little superstition probably can't hurt. But we were raised with more than a little. We had medals of all kinds to ward off evil. It was a bit like wearing garlic to ward off Dracula. The medals had special power if they were blessed by a priest, more power if they were blessed by a bishop, and great power if blessed by the pope himself. My twin brother almost died because of such a medal. As infants, we both had Sacred Heart medals pinned to our clothing. My brother broke off the medal and put it in his mouth. He began to choke on it and would have died had not my mother heard the choking. She hit him on the back and the medal popped out. I don't think we had many more medals pinned to us.

And what about relics? We still have pieces of

bones, clothing, and such from many of the saints.
We even have the tongue of St. Anthony preserved
on a golden spike in the basilica at Padua, Italy. It's
all a bit bizarre. We begin to get involved in some sort
of cosmic game, trying to see which relic is stronger,
which saint can do more. It's the Greek Pantheon all
over again. Assuming God is busy or not listening,
we try to use intermediaries to accomplish what we
want. We believe the saints will be able to get God's
attention better than we can.

At St. Peter's in Chicago, many people will bring in
small statues of St. Joseph to be blessed. The reason
for so many blessed statues has little to do with devo-
tion. The superstition making the rounds is that if
you bury a blessed statue of St. Joseph upside down
in your yard, you will sell your house faster. Some
people even hear the story from their realtors. So
when people present me with a small statue of St.
Joseph to be blessed, I will sometimes ask them if
they intend to bury it. Many admit that's what they
are going to do. But, not to worry, they will dig the
statue up again when they have sold their house. It
certainly makes you wonder.

At St. Peter's, I wound up blessing all kinds of
things. There's a religious goods store in the base-
ment of the church. People would purchase something and then bring it up to the office to have
it blessed. Now I believe in blessings. Food can be
blessed as a sign of thanksgiving. People can be
blessed as a way of showing care and concern. But I
wonder about blessing things, as if to give them special power. I continue to do it, but I'm not happy

about it. It's the same feeling I get when it comes time to bless throats in honor of St. Blase. It makes me feel like some sort of magician or wizard. Do we really believe we'll avoid illnesses of the throat with a St. Blase's blessing? Do we really believe we'll have a better chance of winning if we play with blessed baseball bats?

I'm not trying to belittle these practices. They were part of my childhood and are easy to understand from the viewpoint of a child. The question is why we continue these practices as adults. Do they make us feel "protected"? Can God's power be bought and sold with a relic or blessing? Will medals ward off evil? If evil could be handled so easily, I would be the first to resume medal-wearing. But the protection which comes from God is not the kind which can be bought or sold or manipulated.

God's grace, in a sense, protects us all. Most of us live lives which can be spoken of as "charmed." But it's something extended to all life. When evil breaks through, it shouldn't come as a surprise. We should be thankful for the protection we do get. I don't want to imply that God's grace can be manipulated. But we can open up to it, like a flower opening to the sun.

Another way we attempt prayer is by lighting candles. As long as the candle burns, our prayer is "rising" to God. I remember being fascinated with these candles, these "vigil lights," when I was a child. My mother would light one every so often when we had something or someone special to pray for. The candles created a beautiful, magical effect in the church; the flickering lights in their red containers. I still like the effect they create. I have been in many churches where the burning candles gave a sense of peace to the place. But do they make God more likely to listen to our prayers? What I believe they can do is help us turn inward. They can help create a spirit of prayer within us. And that's surely important. But many of us keep lighting candles, expecting a quicker answer to what we seek.

St. Peter's is the only church I know of which has electric vigil lights. Press a button and on they come. I admit preferring the real candles for effect. But hundreds and hundreds of people keep lighting the electric vigil lights. Maybe they feel it's something practical to do in the face of whatever crisis they're facing. They get their alloted time (the lights are on timers) and it helps them to feel a bit better. Religion should help people feel better. But it shouldn't promise more than it can deliver. By accepting the money which people put in the light offering box, what, if anything, is being promised in return? If we're only helping the person find a little solace in the midst of their troubles, that's fine. If we're helping the person achieve a spirit of prayer, that's fine, too. But if we seem to be offering more, then we must be careful. I like vigil lights. I'm just a bit confused about what they mean.

I think we need sacred places to help us pray. Churches, deserts, forests, mountaintops, all have a history of being places where the sacred is more easily encountered. Such places help us respond to God's touch. But it's not God who needs these places. It doesn't matter to God whether we pray in a church or in a forest. God is no more present in a church than in our own homes. But when we get used to a place, it sometimes loses its "specialness." We begin to take it for granted. And when something (or someone) is taken for granted, then it's hard to enter into a spirit of prayer because prayer is often connected with a sense of thankfulness.

So we come to our churches, seeking the God who seems to evade us elsewhere. And while it's important for us to come together to worship, our worship doesn't make God more present. God is not under our command, rushing about when we demand his presence. What happens when we pray and when we worship is we become more capable of seeing and hearing. We open to God's ever-present presence.

There are times when young people will come up and tell me that they don't see any reason for church. They tell me they find it easier to pray in the woods. I tell them I'm happy they can pray in the woods. The woods are also one of my favorite places to pray. But I also tell them that Christianity is not a "personal" religion but, rather, a "social" one. We are people who join together to seek and to search. We are not seeking a "me and God" kind of holiness. Our holiness is achieved through the ways we treat each other. St. John makes it clear in his first letter that we cannot say we love God if we hate our neighbor. And if we believe God is love, then we make him more present to our world through the love we have for each other. We need to come together and we also need to be alone.

When I was growing up, I came to assume that God

listened better if the prayer was in Latin. His main language was surely Latin. English would still work, but it wasn't as "powerful." I liked Latin. It fascinated me as a child. When I became an altar boy, I delighted in being able to respond in Latin. But as I was finishing high school, the mass began to be fully celebrated in English. By that time, however, I was no longer fascinated with Latin. Having studied it for four years, I realized my ineptitude for the language. I was happy I wouldn't have to say mass in Latin. I was happy that my studies in philosophy and theology would be in English. Up to that time, those studies had been taught mostly in Latin.

Certainly God "hears" all languages. He becomes equally present to someone speaking Chinese or Finnish. He is father to all his children. It doesn't matter to him if we're able to speak Polish or Serbo-Croatian or no language at all. God is beyond language, beyond nationality. But this message isn't always believed. Not long ago, for instance, the leader of the Southern Baptist Conference made an incredible statement. He claimed God didn't hear the prayers of Jews. The reaction to this unbelievable statement was overwhelming. The poor man had to apologize shortly afterward. Yet think about it: God's own son was a Jew. To be fair, we all say things we later regret. But I'm afraid that this attitude has deep roots in some established churches.

What is prayer supposed to be anyway? By turning to prayer, we admit we don't have all the answers. We admit that we are struggling to understand. Maybe something bad has happened. We pray, trying to see some point to the suffering. Prayer also changes us from who we think we are into who we really are. Prayer, especially in the form of ritual, evokes a struggle within us. Forces which don't often appear in our ordinary lives clash within us, helping us to unfold. Prayer helps us to recognize the ever-present touch of God, a touch so deep inside that we usually overlook it.

We need to be aware of what we are attempting with our prayers. Prayer doesn't cause God to know our needs. As Jesus told us: "In your prayer, do not rattle on like the pagans. They think they will win a hearing by the sheer multiplication of words. Do not imitate them. *Your Father knows what you need before you ask him.*" As children, our prayers did a lot of asking. As adults, our prayers should be of a different sort. They should help us to become more and more open to mystery. Our prayers should help us fashion new eyes and new ears. How we pray says a great deal about who we think we are praying to.

Chapter Five
OUR GOD IS OFTEN TOO SMALL

IS God God for everyone? The answer seems obvious, but there are times when we don't accept the obvious answer. We like to make God our own. He belongs to our race, our ethnic group, our church, our religion, our nation. This "making God our own" becomes very evident in war. When we go to war, we assume God is on our side. Our enemies are his enemies. God "grants" us victory. In the same way, the Israelites believed God was leading them into battle, helping them slay the enemy. Losing in battle could only be caused by sin.

We Americans often believe that God is an advocate of the democratic way. He wants us to be victorious over the communists, who are not loved as we are. We Catholics put American flags in our churches to show that being Catholic doesn't make us any less patriotic. My classmates and I removed the flags that were in the church where we were to be ordained. We put them back after the ordination. But perhaps it's time for them to be permanently put away. Being Catholic means being catholic.

Whenever a religion pictures God as leaning toward a certain group, then that religion has some sickness in it. The degree of sickness depends on the degree God is seen as favoring certain peoples. It's a natural reaction, but one which gets in the way of healthy religion. It's like asking a father or mother which of their children they love the most. A parent may very well have "favorites," but God loves us all the same. His love may become more evident in certain people, but that doesn't mean God loves them more. Yet we all want to be "favorites." Whether it's in trying to win a special place with our parents or in fashioning a special niche with our religion, we all strive to stand out from the crowd. But if our religion gives us the impression of being "above" our fellow humans, then our religion is dangerous.

The Israelites believed they were special. God had especially chosen them. They were able to destroy their enemies and conquer the "Promised Land." God was on their side. But look at the story of Jonah. Jonah wants God to destroy all the people of Nineveh. When God doesn't destroy them, Jonah gets upset. God asks Jonah why all those people should be destroyed since they are also his children. God is God not only for the Israelites but for their enemies as well.

Sometimes, however, we "overlook" the message of Jonah. We turn instead to the message found in such places as the Psalms. The Psalms are prayers and songs which relate much of the Israelites' history. They also make up the main portion of the Divine Office, which is supposed to be said daily by priests and religious. Many Psalms call for the destruction of the enemy. The Psalms also talk about bashing children against walls and other such brutalities. They present a vindictive and warlike God. Certainly, there is much beauty to be found in the Psalms, but the beauty is often clouded by the destructive elements. God is pictured as being on my side. He will crush my enemies. Such ideas have little place in a healthy religion.

I have brought up my problems with praying the Psalms at a couple of clergy meetings. I am usually looked at as someone who has either lost his faith or is in grave danger of such a loss. I am told not to take the appearance of the "War God" too seriously. But why should anyone bother with prayers that can't be taken seriously? I have also been told that I am not looking deep enough. That's certainly possible. Yet I continue to have difficulties with the Psalms.

What about war? Does God choose sides? Won't God be on the side of "right"? Look at the Second World War. Surely Hitler was a grave danger to the peoples of the world. His destruction of the Jewish people, along with all the other millions who died, was an unspeakable horror. But in our war with Hitler, did we believe God to be on our side? If we did, then our image of God was too small. We would have been asking God to choose between his children. We would have been asking him to help destroy his own sons and daughters. But could we love and worship a father who would murder his own children?

We have often made our enemies "godless." We fight against people who are not Christian and assume God will be on our side. History is filled with such thinking and the destruction unleashed because of it. Moslems, Hindus, Christians, and so on, have all used God in this way. Look at the horror of the

Crusades. Millions have been killed in "religious" wars.

How could we possibly believe in a God who would take sides? Yet how often we've tried to make God our own. God is ours. He isn't yours. And because he's ours, we're better than you. Protestants imagine themselves to be better than Catholics. Catholics imagine themselves to be better than Protestants. Christians imagine themselves to be better than non-Christians. Believers imagine themselves to be better than nonbelievers. It goes on and on. Graveyards are full of the results of the violence which accompanies such thinking.

Can we pray going into battle? Surely we can pray for protection, for life. But we must be careful about praying to God and asking him to destroy the "enemy." We misuse the idea of God when we pray in such a way. Look at what happens if we win a war or battle. Don't we thank God? But what are we thanking God for? Are we giving thanks that the killing is finished or are we giving thanks that God helped us to win the war?

Many of us would like to believe that God helped us win. Many of us would like to believe that God helped us to return from battle. Our friends and comrades may have been killed, but God kept us alive because we're somehow special to him. Yet what are we doing when we claim God's special intervention in our lives? Can we believe God would allow others to die, while saving us from destruction? What kind of God would pick and choose between those who would return from battle and those who would not?

God wants us all to live. It's just our need to feel special which claims more than it should. We would like to believe God reached down and kept us safe. But why wouldn't he keep the others safe as well? We want to believe it's because we're special to God and he has something left for us to do. We would like to believe it's more than fate. Yet during the Second World War, Hitler escaped a number of attempts on his life. Was God protecting him? He was protecting him as much as everyone else. In God's house, there are no favorites, all are special.

My twin brother fought in Vietnam. He endured many life-threatening situations. He survived and returned home. I was delighted. I gave thanks to God. But I also knew God had not chosen my brother to return while allowing others to die. God doesn't control things in that way. There were many praying for my brother's return. Such prayers may have been a special embrace to him in danger. Yet if God were able to choose which soldier would die and which would come home, then he would have them all return safely. If God were able to have a hand in war, he would keep anyone from falling in battle. But the cost of the freedom which God has given us is the evil which sometimes breaks out in war. God cannot do a great deal about it without taking away our freedom, which he won't do.

In the last discourse before his death, Jesus prayed that all might become one as he and the Father were one. The main prayer of the Christian Church, therefore, should be a prayer of unity. One of her main tasks should be the work of unity. But our history, unfortunately, hasn't been one of working for unity. The church has often divided people. Since the time of Constantine, Western religion has often wielded the sword of intolerance.

Constantine had a dream in which he was told to place the sign of the cross on the shields of his soldiers. He then won the Battle of the Milvian Bridge. Having won the battle, Constantine made Christianity the official religion. It was no longer punishable by death. But as Christianity became more and more accepted it also became less and less tolerant. The less tolerant it became, the more it built up walls for protection. Those who threw stones against the wall were either excommunicated or burned. The church became a devouring mother instead of a loving one.

There were understandable reasons for this "siege mentality." Most of Europe was disintegrating. There were ferocious attacks from all sides. Civilization, as it was known, was on the brink of extinction. But the church was able to endure and became the predominant force in Western Europe. She became supreme power and with that power came the subsequent corruption. The more power was sought, the less love was present.

The way I was raised, I believed the church could do no wrong. The church was incapable of mistakes. That's what I thought infallibility was about. But growing up with such a notion is like growing up with the idea that one's parents are infallible. Children need to see their parents as human, prone to mistakes. Children also need to learn that the church is capable of mistakes, that she is also human. Otherwise, we'll end up with a lopsided image which we'll have to defend against any challenge. A lot of energy can be wasted in such meaningless struggle. With expectations of a perfect church, we wind up with people who say "My religion, right or wrong!" and those who suffer disillusionment. We wind up with defenders and defectors. It leads to a lot of pain.

I know I didn't accept priesthood in order to defend anything. I accepted priesthood in order to pursue truth and to help others in the same pursuit. I was ordained in order to open myself as best I could to the experience of God and to help others do the same. The fact that I work within the structures of the Catholic Church is secondary. Sometimes I enjoy working within those structures, sometimes I do not. But being Catholic is what I am. I happen to find much of what I need within the church. But the church is not primary, God is.

If we believe that church is primary, we focus on the church and not on God. We begin to compete with other churches over potential members. We claim to have special revelations, special truths. We begin to look on other churches as enemies. We call them names and brand them as heretics or heathens. And then the poison of religious racism sickens the world. As Paul Tournier points out in *The Whole Person in a Broken World:* "The great problem of our time is to restore men's faith in a solidarity that transcends all differences of opinions. The world will not listen to the church as long as it does not successfully apply itself to the resolving of its own divisions. . . . Let the Catholics be truly Catholic. Let the

Protestants be truly Protestant. Let the members of
the Salvation Army be true warriors for salvation.
But let spiritual unity be established among all Christians."

There are many roads that lead to God. Tolerance
is crucial. I may have theological or philosophical
problems with some of the roads, but I must be willing to let others find their path. For me to impose a
path on someone else leads only to tyranny. As long
as a religion helps a person to grow and to find their
freedom, then it is a path worth pursuing.

That doesn't mean all paths are open. Surely some
of the "cults" which proliferate today are highly dangerous. They take away what is best and most human
from their members. My sense of religious tolerance
doesn't extend to roads which deadend. Surely any
religion which takes away freedom should be exposed. But one must be careful here. Knowledge is
important for discerning. Just because we may prefer
a well-worn path doesn't mean it's the best for everyone else.

We Catholics have tended to be a bit too protective
in the past. We hid our church's blemishes or de-
fended them as beauty marks. Other churches have
done the same. We have been engaged in some sort
of "beauty contest." But the result of this "contest"
has been religious racism. That's what happens
when we must defend our religion instead of sharing
it. To share our religion, we must be willing to
tolerate questions and doubts. Facts will be brought
up which may make us uneasy. Most of us weren't
given much in the way of theology. We were taught

to accept what we were told. Either we believed or we didn't. There was little room for debate.

Because of this unwillingness to debate, the church began to seem removed from ordinary life. Church was something we did on Sunday which didn't affect the rest of our week. Clergy were seen as people unaccustomed to the ways of the world. The sermons we heard rarely spoke to the heart of human difficulties. The church seemed to be "other worldly," unconcerned with what was going on here and now. I'm exaggerating this point. Surely there have always been good men and women working in the church to keep real problems front and center. But these people have been and will continue to be the exceptions.

The way we treat our clergy may be one of the reasons for the problem. My mother, born and raised in Ireland, would have to get off the sidewalk if a priest was coming toward her. She could not presume to share the sidewalk with the priest and would have to get off into the street. Priests were looked at with either awe or disdain.

We keep our priests in rectories, which become quasi-prisons. Rectories are very seldom "homey." There is often a staff to take care of things. When I moved into the rectory in Parma, Ohio, I was told I could leave my door open in the morning and someone would clean my bedroom and make my bed. I could leave my laundry by the door and it would be washed. My meals would be taken care of by the cook. Now I'm not denying the need for help in taking care of rectories, but all these little "privileges" can keep the priest from feeling ordinary. When that happens, he becomes removed from the center of the human heart. I think it's good for priests to do their own laundry and do some of their own cooking and cleaning. It keeps one human. Otherwise priests can feel like "kept" men.

By treating our priests as "special," we place them apart from us. The results are unfortunate. We dress them up in special clothes. We make them asexual. We put them up in houses removed from other people. So why wonder when their sermons don't deal with ordinary human experiences? How can they preach about human concerns when we don't treat them as human? The more privileges and considerations we give them, the more we strip them of their humanity. And, while it's nice avoiding speeding tickets and receiving discounts, the price is really much too high.

By making our priests and religious into "special" people, perhaps we're trying to make our religion more special. But a path is only as good as the people who walk on it. Being Catholic is special, but so is being Protestant, so is being Buddhist, so is being Moslem, so is being a nonbeliever.

Are there differences between religions? Surely there are. But because each person is special, so is the way they attempt to return to God. It's people who are important. Religions are merely the tools we use to climb to God. Some tools are better for climbing than others. Some tools fit some people better than others.

Religion should help us to become community. It should help feed the hunger we have for each other.

We are social creatures. We need contact. There are very few of us built for isolation. Religion should bring us together, speaking again and again about the worldwide sisterhood-brotherhood which is our calling. If life is found on other worlds, then it must include that life as well. God is God of all life. If religion is meant to bring us closer to God, then it must bring us closer to all life.

Religion has to do with achieving openness. If our religion closes us off to any section of humanity, or even any form of life, then it is unhealthy. If being Catholic turns us against Protestants, then there is something wrong. If being Christian turns us against those who are not Christian, then we have gone astray. If our religion fills us up with even a small amount of hatred or prejudice, then it may be doing us more harm than good.

I mentioned earlier that the universe is estimated to be some 12 billion light years across. It's an enormous place. When the Israelites began to experience God, the universe was thought to be infinitely smaller. Through most of her 2,000 year history, the Christian Church believed the earth to be the center of the universe, around which all things revolved. Since we imagined ourselves to be the best products of creation, it was logical to assume we would be at the center. Consider what happened to Galileo when he disputed our center space. The church fought against being removed from the cosmic center. Yet don't we all fight against being taken from center stage?

What religion can do is help us see that life itself is

the center stage. Nothing else is as important. Being off to one side in our galaxy doesn't make God love us any less. God's love overwhelms us no matter where in our universe we might find ourselves. The love is what's important. The place doesn't matter very much.

Since God's love is so enormous, the love we are taught in religion should also strive to be enormous. Religion should help our love to grow as wide and as deep as it can. Maybe we can't imagine the scope of the universe, but we can deal with our own town or city. We can expand our love into the corners of our own world. We can include all people as our brothers and sisters. We can move beyond our own ethnic group, beyond our own race, and see the connections we have with all who live on our planet.

Religions, especially Christianity, should be very vocal about the sins of racism, proclaiming equality always. A man or woman living in the slums of Calcutta is equal to a person living in Beverly Hills. This should be one of the foremost messages of Christianity, reflecting the universal love which God has for all his children. If we dare to call ourselves his children, then all who share our humanity must be included.

Just preaching the message, though, isn't enough. The church must strive to put this message into practice. This means that all people in the church are to be considered equal: male, female, young, old. But the church still has work to do. Is it not cruel, for instance, that a little boy can be an altar server, while his sister is refused? What does one tell a little girl who asks why she can't be a server like her brother?

I'm sorry also for the women who could serve the church in priesthood yet are denied it. Surely it has been a tradition to have an all-male clergy in the church, but there are no significant reasons to continue the tradition. There are no scriptural roadblocks to women's ordination. The church no longer holds to an anti-feminine bias in theology.

There are women studying alongside male students in a number of our Catholic theology schools. They are getting the required education. They just happen to have the wrong sexual apparatus. Mother Church seems to have some jealous feelings concerning her daughters. Hopefully, it will be short-lived. The church can only strike people as lacking credibility if she preaches equality, yet fails to practice it.

Everything living is special. All life is sacred. Religion should teach us this. Sometimes it doesn't. I remember preaching one weekend at a parish in Indianapolis. The parish had a wide reputation for the quality of its liturgies. I was happy to be there. Before one of the masses, one of the parish priests was telling me what they did for their Easter celebration. They had released dozens of butterflies into their church. Since the butterfly has often been used as an Easter symbol, I thought it was a lovely idea. I then asked how they got the butterflies out of the church. The priest replied that they didn't. The butterflies had been left to die. I felt the symbol disintegrate.

Saying that our sense of community needs to expand to include all life doesn't rule out the feelings we have towards smaller groups. Certainly we feel a special closeness to our families, the people in our neighborhood, our ethnic group, our church group. It's natural and desirable to feel affinity with the groups of which we are a part. I feel a special closeness to my Franciscan family. This feeling of "belonging" is even more important today than in the past. Today it's harder to feel part of a group and to feel secure. Some researchers feel our contemporary stress comes significantly from a lack of community connections.

The sense of closeness we feel with these groups, however, shouldn't close us off. Our groups shouldn't make us afraid of other groups. By learning how to love within the small groups, we learn how to love in larger groups. That's if the group is a healthy one. Unhealthy groups make their members prisoners, chaining them with fear and guilt. Close-knit groups are essential, but we must not allow them to suffocate us.

The church sometimes created the impression that what lay outside her realm was all evil and darkness. Salvation could be found only within the church. This notion was condemned as a heresy. Yet it seems many people were given an impression very close to this heresy. I vividly recall feeling sorry for the Protestant boy I mentioned in the beginning. I just knew he wouldn't be able to get to heaven. I don't know where the idea came from, but it couldn't have been invented solely in my mind. It was somehow planted there.

The groups we belong to give us some of our sense of identity. Difficulty arises, however, when the group identity overwhelms. If the church causes us to believe we have no identity apart from her, then we have landed in a snare. We need to understand that there is salvation apart from the church. The church is important. It helps us to put down roots where we can blossom. But God would still love us if there were no church. God would still love us if we were Buddhist or Moslem, believer or nonbeliever.

God is not Catholic. He is not Moslem. He is not American. He is not Russian. He is not white. He is not black. He is not brown. He is not red. He is not yellow. He is not what we want him to be. Yet most of us keep trying to make him our own. Those of us who are white think of God as being white. Those of us who are black think of God as being black. And so on. We picture Jesus in similar ways. But in trying to describe God in terms of our racial or national character, we distort his image. Is it impossible to present God without such human colorings? It's possible but difficult. Again we can use the concepts found in St. John's Letters: God is light and love. We need to further develop our God language. God is not an old man sitting on a cloud, off in the heavens. To use such descriptions with our children can only keep them from finding God in their lives.

Sometimes the church tries to control God. The church claims to speak for God in our world. But we must be cautious. There are times when I am preaching that I feel filled with something special. It might be an inner conviction about what I am saying. It might be a deep feeling for the message. Yet I would never claim to be speaking for God. My words may on special occasions help someone to experience God. That would be the most I could hope for, and it's a lot to hope for.

Many of us, though, who are priests and preachers believe that God puts words in our mouths. What we say from our pulpits is considered a direct communication from God. It's the same understanding some of us have regarding Scripture. We speak of Scripture as being "inspired by God." I believe in inspiration. The image many of us have, however, is of God dictating the words while some quasi-secretary writes them down. Such an image of inspiration does a great disservice to Scripture. The same kind of disservice is done when any church or minister claims to be God's direct messenger. God will not be controlled.

Yet the attempts to control keep happening. There are a number of ministers who like to declare who's going to get it next from God. They speak of God "rolling up his sleeves," getting ready to do business with gays or liberals or communists or whoever. God is pictured as some sort of celestial boxer, always ready to punch out somebody's lights. How could we possibly believe in such a God? Yet how easy it seems to rally people around the claim of coming divine retribution. "God's going to wipe out all our enemies. Just wait!" The God of Vengeance has deep roots in our thinking and in our history.

Whenever a preacher or church leader claims "God's on our side!" we can be sure they're trying to control God and us in the process. Whenever anyone shouts out some coming divine punishment, we can be sure they're misguided. And whenever God's name is used to make money, we can be sure his name is being misused. Religion should not be in the business of making money. Churches and church schools are expensive. They need to be supported if we want them to continue. But to claim that God wants us to support the churches or the schools is just untrue. God needs neither our churches nor our schools. We need them.

We need to be careful about how money is gathered for our churches. To say God expects us to give 10 percent of what we earn to the church (or any percentage) is just wishful thinking from church accountants. For a preacher or a priest to demand money in God's name is appalling. I've sat in churches where the contributions of the members were read from the pulpit. I wonder what God must be thinking. It happens in Christian churches. It happens in non-Christian churches. Look at what theologian John L. McKenzie points out in his *Did I Say That?*: "It is simply not conceivable that Jesus ever meant to establish anything which would enable men systematically to exploit him for profit." When it does happen, we have unhealthy religion. If people see the reason for churches, they will support them. If no reason for their existence is acknowledged, then they will fade away.

Many priests, especially pastors, are concerned with the financial situation of their local parishes. Many good men spend a major part of their time wrestling with money concerns. It's truly unfortu-

nate. Priests need not be business managers. There
are enough people who have such training. There are
enough important homilies to be given without
spending even one on money worries. I recognize
that finances are important. People give generously
to many churches. But if people are unwilling to
spend the significant funds needed for Catholic
schools, then let them close. If their value is not evident, then why should they be supported?

I am a product of many years of Catholic education. I am grateful for Catholic schools. I hope they
are able to continue long into the future. But they
have also become an enormous burden to many parishes. Parish schools utilize most of the money col-
lected in their parishes. And whose job is it to collect
all this money? If the pastor or parish priests accept
the responsibility, then they will have much less
energy and time for other ministries. This financial
albatross is hanging around the necks of many who
minister in the church. It has had a debilitating effect
on the life of the church. It also has no easy solution.

Anyway, these are just a few of the ways we make
God too small. We try to grab hold of God, yet he
always eludes us. We need to pursue God (and let
ourselves be "pursued" by him), but we can never
claim capture. Churches have sometimes given the
impression that such capture was accomplished:
God could be found in our church but not in any
other. No church is closer to God's heart than any
other. To make such a claim means that God favors
some people more than others. It's this idea of
"favoring" which causes so much trouble. God's love

cannot be increased because of any church membership. We can't win any more of God's love by joining a certain church.

What can happen, though, is that we might become more open to God's love because of the ministry and activity of a certain church. I first came to know of God's love for me through the ministry of the Catholic Church. That doesn't mean I wouldn't have found God's love in some other church. But I am eternally thankful for what I have discovered within the structure of the Catholic Church. Surely, people can also discover God's love outside of any church. Churches may even get in the way of the discovery from time to time. But God's love always continues to be there, waiting to be found. It will outlast every church.

God is bigger than we can imagine. He is found everywhere in our vast universe. His love bathes every nook and cranny of creation. The farthest planet in the farthest galaxy is swept up in his love. To claim a special piece of that love is unnecessary. There is more than enough to go around. Yet it is human nature to try to horde it. Religions have continually tried to claim it as their sole possession. Yet his love just keeps rolling like the proverbial river. God doesn't belong to any church or any religion. Everything belongs to him. Sometimes we forget.

Chapter Six
WHAT DOES A HEALTHY RELIGION LOOK LIKE?

MANY of the religious ideas we were raised with led to unhealthy notions about God and religion. Can religion help us to have the broadness of mind and heart needed to become fully human? I believe it can. But first we must acknowledge that our religion, be it Catholic or whatever, can keep us from questioning. Just as we learn at an early age the subjects to avoid with our parents, so we learn to avoid certain questions regarding our religion. Maybe some of the questions we raised when we were young, in Catholic grade school or in our religious instruction, weren't really answered. Maybe we were given the feeling that to question was dangerous. But a healthy religion not only welcomes questions, it seeks them. Since understanding is part of the task of religion, questions are essential.

We need to question our priests, our sisters, our bishops, our ministers, and each other. Dialogue helps us to grow. Too often we have kept to the easy path, avoiding difficult questions. Yet religion is about searching. And one cannot search without the proper tools. Just as digging is best done with a shovel, so searching is best done with an open heart and a questioning mind. If religion attempts to quiet questions, then it is unhealthy. If we are afraid to bring our beliefs into the light of examination, then our beliefs might be enslaving us rather than setting us free.

Certainly faith is needed. Faith is first and foremost the experience of God. Such an experience may come when we suffer an enormous loss. It may come when we behold the grandeur of creation. It may come in the midst of a moving liturgy. It may come in a quiet moment of love. Faith is that awakening to God's presence that we try to understand with our questions, with our searching. The medieval philosophers and theologians spoke of "faith seeking understanding." We seek a similar understanding. Faith is not adherence to a set of laws that we have been ordered to obey. Faith goes beyond creedal proclamations. We "taste and see the goodness of the Lord."

What about the church laws that we were raised with? Are they important? Yes and no. They're important because they help shape our religious community. Religious anarchy is no better than any other form of anarchy. Laws and regulations give structure to our religious pursuits. But they are not *that* important! The laws are not more important than the people who believe in them. Religious freedom demands that we not be overwhelmed with an exorbitant number of rules and regulations. Otherwise, the more rules and regulations there are, the more our religious landscape becomes a swamp where we will get trapped.

Let's take a look at the Catholic obligation for Sunday worship. Sunday mass is important. It's important to worship and to worship together. But the obligation of Sunday attendance isn't that crucial. There would be some who would be upset if the church dropped obligatory Sunday attendance. Many parents might wonder how they could keep getting their children to Sunday mass. Yet what kind of weapon does the church have to force people to mass? If we go to mass because the church says we'll go to hell if we miss, then we remain moral adolescents.

If a person doesn't want to be at mass, then it might be better for all of us if that person wasn't there. Sunday mass would no longer be an obligation that needs to be "gotten over with." We wouldn't have so many people searching for a priest who was "fast." It's also true our churches might become a good deal emptier than they are now.

Should we teach our children religion at all? Yes, indeed. But not in the same way that most of us were taught. Should we bring them to church? Yes, church should be a family celebration. Yet mass can be very difficult for our young ones. Most of the time they can't even see what's happening. I like to bring the small ones up around the altar when possible, because if mass isn't something our young ones find rewarding, then how can we expect them to continue attending when the choice is fully theirs? It's a very difficult area. I don't have solutions. I do know, though, that the age when we can force people into church is drawing to a necessary end. This doesn't mean mass and other liturgies have to become "en-

tertaining." It does mean that they will have to be
moving. They will have to help people reach out to
God and reach out to each other.

Why would any of us who were raised Catholic go
to church if we weren't "forced"? Well, either
church speaks to our needs and struggles or it
doesn't. If we aren't aware of the emptiness within
us, then we will find little in church. Church is a
place to ponder the eternal questions, to ask about
meaning. But if there are no questions in our lives,
then there is little reason to enter a church. Healthy
religion helps us ask the questions. It doesn't claim to
have the answers, only fragments and clues. Religion
is like an old pirate's map, pointing the way to buried
treasure. Religion nourishes us with the food without
which our spirits would starve.

I have found this nourishment in the Catholic
Church. Being Catholic is important to me. Many of
my ancestors suffered for their religion. I would not
be anything but what I am. Yet I am also aware that
many who were raised Catholic have turned to other
religions or no religion at all. They might still marry
in the church and have their children baptized, but
it's often done to appease their families. It usually
makes me sad. It makes me sad because so many of
us were not helped to see the beauty of the church.
We found ourselves feeling imprisoned, looking for
escape.

Part of the problem is that the church tried to cover
over her blemishes. She became a woman with too
much make-up on. No make-up is better than too
much. So what if our church has blemishes? Why

should we expect or demand perfection from her? If the church would allow her true face to be seen, we could see her beauty and humanity. Many of us Catholics have never glimpsed the church's real face and that's a tragedy. The church's face reflects the beauty of one who has aged well. There are lines and wrinkles, but they are a delight to behold, speaking as they do of sunny days and smiles and tears.

The church has often hidden her face by trying to have all the answers. Maybe she was fearful that we would see the doubt written into her face. Maybe she felt we wouldn't love her if we saw that doubt. But why should we expect the church to have all the answers? No church has all the answers. And I think most of us would rather see the human lines of doubt than a rigid and inhuman certitude.

A healthy religion also has a sense of humor. One of the biggest complaints I have against religion is that it so often seems humorless. How often have we laughed in church, or even smiled? Sometimes when I'm preaching, I'll say something funny, but there is usually little response. Maybe what I say isn't all that humorous, but it does seem that religion is overly stern. A healthy religion should be able to laugh at itself, chuckling over its own missteps. I find religion to be continually amusing. For instance, I don't have to be very long in a confessional before I start smiling to myself. When people confess that they "entertained impure thoughts," I always imaging them taking the thoughts out for dinner or a night on the town. Where does one take an impure thought to entertain it?

A healthy religion should give us the strength to change who we are. It should encourage us to give up destructive ways of behaving. We all need to be pointed in the right direction when we get lost. It also helps to have a compass. It's so easy to get lost in life. A healthy religion provides us with a type of compass.

Rather than preventing us from entering places where there are few signposts, religion should guide us when we ask for it. The church probably shouldn't try to guide those who don't want guidance. Not much is accomplished that way. Yet the church has sometimes tried to do that in the past. But if a person doesn't feel lost, it does little good trying to convince them they are lost. That's like condemning the world in order to save it.

A healthy religion helps us become more and more a part of life. This task is even more essential today when so many of us are becoming spectators in our own lives. We spend so many hours watching television, becoming passive, letting others experience life as we look on. Religion can be the net under the high wire. The net is there for when we fall, but its whole purpose and reason for being is to get us up on the high wire. A healthy religion teaches us to climb up to the high wire. It teaches us how to live.

A healthy religion has to do with life. That's simple enough but not always understood. For instance, look at the reaction to Andrew Greeley's novels: *The Cardinal Sins, Thy Brother's Wife, Ascent into Hell,* and *Lord of the Dance.* There has been outrage from many places because the novels contained sexual passages, while also showing the humanness of the church. I found all four novels to be delightful, as well as encouraging to my own priesthood. It's a pity so many avoided the novels because of silly ideas promulgated by people who find it difficult to laugh at themselves. I've lost track of the number of people who either confessed reading these novels (believing such to be sinful) or who asked my permission to read them. I was not ordained to be a censor. The church's business is not one of censorship. Its business is life.

A healthy religion also needs to be involved with the real concerns of people. Certainly the church has done that in many places. It has helped untold millions over the years. But here in the United States, the church has sometimes retreated from the real problems of people. The fault may be partially due to our seminary training. Often seminaries are places removed from ordinary life. In the not-too-distant past, seminarians were discouraged from forming close friendships. Intellectual growth occurred but little emotional growth. Today the situation is better but seminaries are still too "isolated," too removed from life as it's normally lived.

A healthy religion helps us feel part of a larger whole. It helps us sense we are not alone, that there is more to life than we imagine. It unites us to others, yet it doesn't protect us from our aloneness. Being united and being alone are both important experiences for a full life. A healthy religions points out the bridges that can be used in the journey out of one's self. It also helps us find caves when we need to be hermits.

All of us must come to terms with pain and suffering. A healthy religion offers a workable philosophy of pain. It doesn't promise a pain-free life. It doesn't try to justify pain by claiming it to be God's will. Pain and suffering are part of life and we must deal with them. The experience of both can deepen us as people, opening us to a fuller life. We have grown accustomed to avoiding pain. Whenever we feel pain, such as a headache, we reach for something to deaden it. Yet pain has a purpose. It tries to tell us that something is wrong. If we mask the pain through drugs, then we fail to find the reason for the pain. It's not that all pain should be endured rather than medically eased. But pain is essential to our human life. It forces us to listen. It helps us to be honest with ourselves. A healthy religion senses the importance of such honesty.

Not that pain and suffering should be sought for their own sake. There have been plenty of people in the history of the church who pursued pain. Pain was promoted as a way of dealing with the desires of the flesh and coming closer to God. Many people wore hairshirts with metal pieces designed to tear their skin. Look at St. Simeon Stylites, a rather crazy monk who lived in the desert during the fifth century. St. Simeon would wound himself and then place maggots on the wounds to further the suffering. Look at St. Francis of Assisi, whom I admire deeply. He died earlier than he needed because of all the damage he did to his body. It was part of the spirituality of those times to see punishment as a way to holiness. Such an idea has stayed with us until very recent times.

There was a practice known as "discipline" which was practiced in many religious Orders. It was practiced in the Franciscan Order until the mid-1960s. People would take whips and flog themselves. At least once a week those who were in the training year known as novitiate would go to their rooms and "discipline" themselves. Most, of course, didn't take it too seriously. They would beat on their pillows or bed. But some did take it seriously. I'm glad it was dropped a year or two before I entered the novitiate. Can we imagine a God who would want us to beat our own bodies as a sign of worship? Yet our church, along with other churches, sometimes promoted a kind of masochistic spirituality. We all need self-discipline, but not mutilation. Holiness is not best achieved by destroying the body.

A healthy religion also helps people develop their own sense of responsibility. We talked a little about this when we were discussing sin. We all need to create within ourselves an awareness of how we are connected to others. Religion helps us find the right balance between freedom and responsibility. It does that by emphasizing our human connections. We are tied to other people, so we need to be responsible in the ways we deal with each other. We are tied to other life forms as well, so we must also seek responsible ways of dealing with them. Healthy religion makes the connections clear.

Healthy religion should also help us come to terms
with our sexual energies. The church has tended to
either concentrate all her attention on the possible
misuse of sex or ignore the subject altogether. I'm
surprised how infrequently the subject of sexuality is
raised among priests and religious. It's almost a
taboo subject. I'm not suggesting we devote all our
time and energies to its discussion, but certainly sexuality is an important subject in everyone's life, including those who are celibate. Just because one
promises a celibate life doesn't make the energies of
sex diminish. Maybe if those of us who are priests
and religious spent more time in open discussion, we
would be able to fashion a much-needed contemporary theology of sexuality.

Healthy religion helps us to have more self-esteem,
more confidence in ourselves. Too often we fail to
see that if we praise God too much, then we won't
have enough praise left for ourselves. God doesn't
need to be told how wonderful he is, but we do need
to be told. Humility is important. Self-deprecation is
not. Sometimes in our prayers and worship, we diminish the awareness of our own goodness. I am not
a hopeless wretch. I am a man struggling with life.
An awareness of my sinfulness helps me understand
who I am. But an exaggerated sense of sinfulness
only distorts my identity. An appreciation of our
worth opens us to God and to his creation. A sense of
being worthless only shuts the door on life.

"Those who have grown the most spiritually are
those who are the experts in living." (From Peck's
The Road Less Traveled.) A healthy religion helps us

become "experts in living." A healthy church encourages our explorations. In our explorations, we'll make mistakes. We'll get lost at times. The church is there to offer both forgiveness and healing when we are in need of them. But the church, any church, should not put "Off Limits" or "No Trespassing" signs on anything. Such signs only lead to unhealthy restrictions. The church, like any parent, doesn't want her children to get hurt. But just as a healthy parent knows the price of learning to walk includes bumps and bruises, so a healthy religion knows that the price of maturity includes mistakes made and acknowledged. Certainly priests, ministers, and religious teachers can point out some of the dangerous twists and turns in the road, but they should never discourage the journey.

A healthy religion doesn't waste energy boasting about itself. There are many in the church who feel they are "owed something" because of the ministry they perform. Since they have "given up so much," they feel superior to others, even if only in their "humility" and "simplicity." But most of us who work for others do so because of selfish reasons. Our work helps us to feel useful. It helps us to feel we have a special meaning in life. We have been "called." The truth is that we are only normal people, helping others because we find satisfaction in the work. Ministry brings many rewards. We who work in ministry may need to help others more than they need our help.

A healthy religion has good intellectual roots. In other words, it makes sense. The medieval scholars

spent their lives trying to make faith understandable.
Our faith should also attempt to understand itself. It
should appear convincing to someone with intelli-
gence. God does not ask us to turn off our brains
when we come to worship. And while faith takes us
to a realm beyond the rational, a healthy religion
doesn't ask its followers to believe things which are
obviously wrong. We only make fun of God when we
claim something to be true in his name which we
know to be false.

For example, if we claim all of Scripture to be historically accurate, then we must give up our thinking
capacities. The fight that has been going on recently
between creationists and evolutionists often appears
absurd. Religion has sometimes created the impression of being against science. Certainly science is not
our master. It has many inherent flaws which are
often overlooked. But a healthy religion does not ask
its people to shut their eyes or ears to what science
uncovers. A healthy religion is rooted in what is real.
To ask people to believe in the accuracy of a story
like Noah and the Ark is an insult. A healthy religion
doesn't insult the intellect.

A healthy religion also helps us to experience God.
It's the experience of God that transforms us. Religion is the door we use to enter the sacred room. It
helps us to undergo the second birth spoken of by
Jesus to Nicodemus. But this idea of being "born
again" can sometimes be misused. There are some
who use the term to imply a clique of those "saved."
There are those who will ask the question, "Have you
been born again?" without understanding what they

are asking. The birth which Jesus is speaking about has to do with self-discovery. To be "born again" is to become who we really are. We see the illusions we have wrapped around ourselves. We discover our true identity.

A symbol which might be helpful here is the idea of a castle. We are often led to believe that we are like a castle under siege. We must defend ourselves from attack. We surround ourselves with high walls, with a moat and drawbridge. We may even be led to build all kinds of defensive weapons: cannons, pots of boiling oil, catapults. And so, we then sit inside our castle, intent on defending who we think we are. Our ego, with its illusions, wants protection. Our false side walls out life. The new birth has to do with throwing open the drawbridge and tearing down the walls. We see that we are not a castle in need of defending. We recognize that the more defenses we erect, the more we lose ourselves. The experience of God, the experience of his Spirit, scales the walls and breaks open the castle.

Jacob Needleman in his book *Lost Christianity* seeks the core of our Christian faith. He concludes: "If the search for lost Christianity has any meaning at all, it surely must be this: to bring back Christianity as a guide to the search for ourselves." Healthy Christianity, along with healthy religion in general, opens us to ourselves. It helps us listen to the inner voice which speaks our true name. It helps us contact our natural hunger for truth. It helps us pack for the journey. It makes us eager for the road. It leads us into that forest where the Forest Owner waits for us.

If we wish to find God, we need to find ourselves. We are, in the words of St. John, "God's seeds." Divinity has been planted within us. We speak of this divinity as the "soul." But the soul needs to develop. It needs nourishment, just as any seed needs water and sunshine to blossom. A healthy religion is like water and sunshine, helping whatever seeds are within us to grow. A healthy religion takes us on that inward search to find what God has planted. And such a search takes a lifetime.

Healthy religion nourishes what is best in us. Unhealthy religion nourishes what is worst in us. Healthy religion helps us to grow. Unhealthy religion stifles our growth. Healthy religion brings us out into the light. Unhealthy religion keeps us in the dark. Healthy religion touches our heart. Unhealthy religion touches our fears and angers. Healthy religion readies us for God's touch. Unhealthy religion anesthetizes us to that touch.

We need to realize that there is no such thing as a fully healthy religion, nor is there a fully unhealthy one. All religions are a mixture of what is healthy and what is not. Our task is to learn how to discern the one from the other. Sometimes the wisdom of Solomon might be required. But, with practice, the task becomes easier. We used to speak of those who could discern in this way as "prophets." But we are all called to such a prophetic role. Our church needs our prophetic presence.

I do love the Catholic Church, even though I'm aware of some of her flaws. I would hope and pray that she can continue long into the future. But she will need to help us by returning the love which she gave to so many of us when we were young. Maybe there were strange things mixed with her love, but the love was real. Mother Church did give us "Mother Love."

We all know of homes where the love between mother and father seems to radiate, filling the home with love's warmth. We also know of homes where there is a coldness between mother and father, speaking of something lost or never found. The church is like a home somewhere between these two types. The love which she has for the Father doesn't seem very strong, but it is not altogether lost. What we need to do as her children is help her to discover the love she has forgotten. It's not an easy task. Yet if religion is to survive, our task is exactly this, for a healthy religion is, ultimately, a loving one.

Chapter Seven
FINAL THOUGHTS

THERE are problems facing the church. As Matthew Fox says in *On Becoming a Musical Mystical Bear*: "Statistics indicate that fewer and fewer Americans avail themselves of organized religion. But what numbers cannot reveal is that it is very often the most spiritually minded who absent themselves from the churches. The absence of these persons speaks more loudly than do the generally harmless words delivered from Sunday pulpits." Many of our young people are among these "spiritually minded" missing. All one has to do is visit a few parish churches and look around. The reality of those missing young ones will be quite evident. What has become of them?

Many times a parent has asked me to pray for their son or daughter who has "lost the faith." I always feel sad when I see the look of anguish on the parent's face. Often they will wonder aloud what they did wrong, blaming themselves for something beyond their control. To have a child drop from the church usually causes much pain and many family struggles.

I know of many young people who have turned from the West to look for answers in Eastern religions. The "mystery" of the East has its attraction. It seems less tainted with our Western materialism and violence. It sometimes seems a better solution to the religious needs that we all have. And I am certainly glad when people find religious values, wherever they are found. There is much in the East that we need to study. There us much in the East that could broaden our religious understandings. But the Eastern religions have their flaws, as would be expected. The flaws might not seem so apparent because they are at a distance. Maybe the flaws of our church, and of Christianity in general, seem so obvious to our young that they turn elsewhere, seeking something less flawed.

It's true that if we're raised in a certain religion we'll usually be more aware of what's wrong with it than if seen from a distance. It's like being aware of the problems of our own family, which are hidden from outsiders. If we grow up in a family with conflicts, then other families appear more inviting. We want to belong to the family across the street or down the block. Yet if we were able to magically become part of that family, we would discover they also have family conflicts. It's the same with religions. All religions harbor conflicts. All churches have skeletons in their closets.

I have no problem with those who turn to Eastern religions for answers. The fact that so many have turned to the East instead of just giving up on religion altogether speaks very strongly for the existence of religious needs. But what I hope is that these people will share what they learn with those of us who remain in our Western churches. Those who look to the East are not enemies of those who remain rooted in Western theology, and vice versa. We need to share what we find. It's like recognizing the need to return nutrients to the soil from which we grew. If a soil keeps producing crops without nutrients being restored, then the soil will rapidly deteriorate and nothing will grow there. We, who grew from the soil of the Catholic Church, have something of an obligation to restore the nutrients which were used up by our making.

Those who study the East would also do well to study the West. Both are worth examination. There is much beauty to be found in both world views. (I'm greatly simplifying by distilling Eastern and Western thought into two world views.) The East and the West have a need for each other. Both approaches can give strength to the other. So, while it's fine for people to hunt in the East, I do hope they will some- day return to share with us what they have found. I also hope they will look again at the religious values which the West has to offer.

The fear I share with many parents is the fear that their children will get involved in a "cult." The cults have grown by leaps and bounds during the past two decades. Many who were raised Catholic have found their way into them. Perhaps this has resulted from the "breakdown" of authority in traditionally or- ganized churches. We can see it with the Catholic Church. As the Catholic Church began to give more and more freedom to her members, there were many who longed for less freedom. Many of us have a need for strong structures. If we can be relieved of the need for decision making, then we seem to suffer less stress. So, in a sense, we've lost some of our Catholic children to cults because the church has become more open and less authoritarian.

As our families break apart more and more through increased divorce rates and as our traditional religions lose their appeal, our children will suffer more and more. They will feel cast adrift, on a never-ending sea, lost in the waves. It's no wonder and no surprise when some get caught in cults' nets. They are only searching for direction, for someone to tell them what to do and how to achieve fulfillment. Since many of our young don't find the answers in our traditional churches (even though the answers are there), they are easy prey to whatever cult may come upon them. It's as if they're wounded, becoming easy prey for the carnivores.

I'm not sure what the solution is. I do know that our church needs to show more vigorous signs of vitality. It needs to attract good men and women for ministry. Yet how many mothers and fathers today would want their sons to become priests and religious brothers or their daughters to become religious sisters? Not many, I'm afraid. Perhaps that's a symptom of the church's vocation condition.

There are a number of possible explanations for this lack of enthusiasm. Some of them are obvious: the uncertain future of religious life, the requirement of celibacy, the instability of the church. Another possible reason may have to do with the way the church has treated her ex-priests and religious. The lack of charity shown to these people is appalling. Former priests, for instance, are not allowed to minister in any way, even though many would still wish to do so. I'm not speaking about having them minister as priests. That seems to be only a distant possibility. But many of them could serve the church as deacons, just as many married men serve as deacons today. The church would surely benefit from the love so many of them could bring to her. But, mostly, ex-priests are pushed away into the closet, with the hope that they remain there.

I remember the wedding of one of my classmates. He had been a priest for a couple of years when he realized he could not continue. After a time, he decided he would marry. But even with the ecclesiastical permission (which is becoming harder and harder to get), his wedding was a very closed affair. No one was allowed to be at the wedding. It was performed in a locked church. Those of us who were invited had to be content with seeing the couple at the reception afterwards. We all felt sad to have missed the wedding itself.

The church will have to show more compassion to the good men and women who served her, some for many years. The question of optional celibacy and the meaning of religious life will continue to be debated long into the future. But while that debate goes on, charity and understanding will need to be more evident. The church has lost a significant number from the ranks of priests, sisters, and brothers. For example, in my own Franciscan province (a province is a number of states joined together, like a federation), there were ten men ordained as Franciscan priests in 1968. There is only one still in active

ministry. And these would have been the men now
becoming pastors and leaders. The loss will be felt
for a long time to come.

The church will need to be more "alive," as well as
more compassionate, if we want to keep our children
from turning away. The church will need to give people all the freedom they can handle, while still pro-
viding guidance and care. For those who grow best
in an atmosphere of freedom, it should be given to
them. For those who grow best in a more controlled
environment, it should be available. It's certainly difficult to provide diverse "growing conditions," but
the church is capable of such diversity.

The church and Christianity have something, or
rather someone, special in the person of Jesus. Certainly Jesus adds a poetic, prophetic dimension to
the church. But we can get as confused in our images
of Jesus, the God-man, as we do in our images of
God. Many people still believe that the Gospels are a
kind of biography of Jesus, but they are no such
thing. They were written many years after the death
of Jesus and were not meant to describe the historical
Jesus or his ministry. They were meant to portray
Jesus as experienced by the early Christians. It's
possible there was a collection of the sayings of
Jesus, which served as the basis for the Gospels, but
in no way can they be considered biographical treat-
ments. They are much more than that.

It's the experience of Jesus as Christ, the
"Anointed One," which served as the catalyst for the
church. The church would not have been possible
without that experience. And when the Gospels are

seen in this light, they become extra special. They present a very living faith, shining through the treatment of Jesus' life. They really are the "Good News," as their name implies. Yet many, if not most of us have probably never read one of the four all the way through. The church, meaning those of us who belong to it, will not appear very vital unless we share the experience of Jesus, past and present.

As Alan T. Dale points out in *Portrait of Jesus*: "In a study of Wordsworth, a poet is described as 'a man who throws stones at your window (if he is a poet of any power he breaks it).' . . . I began to think of Jesus as 'breaking windows,' 'crossing frontiers,' 'waking people up,' getting words straight so that people can really talk to one another and make 'Yes' mean 'Yes' and 'No' mean 'No.'" So what Jesus did and what he continues to do is throw stones at our windows. If we are lucky, he will break our windows so that fresh air can come in and we can also get out. The early church is filled with such "broken windows." We could use more of them today. But I fear that many of us have installed bullet-proof glass in our windows.

Christianity has never presented itself as an explanation for the way things are. Rather, it presents us with a description of what can be; what we can be. In Christianity we see a life-plan based squarely on the need for love. By following the understanding of Jesus presented in the New Testament, we see that Christianity is a way of responding to life. It's a way of putting more life in our lives.

The church, however, has often focused on what has been instead of what is and what will be. The past is important, but the church has sometimes tried to give new life to the past at the expense of the present. If the church, or any institution, keeps looking over its shoulder, then it will stumble. Often the church is like the old person who keeps telling stories from the past. There is much wisdom in such stories, but they can also become a bit boring.

I wonder about the children being raised in the church today. Will they find her a loving and caring mother or will they find her to be like a kindly grandmother, whom one visits from time to time, but doesn't take too seriously? If these children don't see the beauty of the church, they will naturally turn elsewhere. It's this search for beauty which is part of our religious quest. But I'm afraid that the beauty of the church has been hidden under layers of laws and regulations. The church, at least for many of her years, has been "overdressed." With the help of the Second Vatican Council she was able to cast off some of these clothes, but I fear she is still too dressed for easy and natural movement.

There's a real dilemma here. Many people liked the brocades and jeweled gowns which the church wore. I admired them myself from time to time. The more she casts off these garments, the more some people will object. Yet the church will need to continue to "disrobe." Jogging is best done when little is worn, and the church needs to see that she is in a race for the faith of our children. But the race isn't so much with other churches or religions as it is with disbelief itself. And most of us would be surely sad to see our young with nothing left to believe in. For the less we believe in, the more love escapes us. The less faith we possess, the less we are able to love.

One of the biggest tragedies in our world today is that we are all rapidly becoming skeptics and cynics. We have so many facts at our fingertips, anything can be argued away. We have endured so many scandals and crushing events. Watergate, the assassinations of the Kennedy brothers and Martin Luther King, Jr., the attempted assassinations of President Reagan and Pope John Paul II, all conspire to diminish the flame of faith. It's as if we find the cost of believing too high. We turn from religion because we're afraid it'll be Santa Claus all over again.

We wind up afraid to trust. Our television commercials have told us from an early age to trust what they say. If we wear this kind of perfume, if we buy this kind of car, if we use this kind of toothpaste, then we will be happy. But it doesn't happen and we are left wondering who we can trust. We turn to the church but we find the church, instead of offering solid ground to stand on, seems to be in the same state that we're in. We see the confusion of current theological debates, with all sides claiming to speak "the truth." We wonder if we will ever find land. We have grown tired of treading water.

What the church can do, however, is offer us a lifesaver or life-jacket. Then we won't fear drowning so much. The church can do this by helping us learn how to trust again; not so much in doctrines as in ourselves and in each other. If we are unable to trust in ourselves and in each other, then we will be unable to trust in God. For religion to be healthy, it must help us trust in a world that seems untrust-worthy.

Our young are especially vulnerable to this untrust. They see so much from such an early age. Television brings so much violence and inhumane behavior into our lives. We, who are older, can help filter and diffuse this dark side of human reality. But our young have not developed such defenses. They are subjected to the full dose, like being irradiated without protection. They see too much too soon.

Yet, even those of us who are not young suffer some consequences. We learn to disbelieve sermons about the goodness of humanity because our television news speaks too loudly about the badness of humanity. We don't really listen to sermons about love because we have become skeptical about love's existence. Skepticism suffocates love. Cynicism or long-lived skepticism poisons love.

So how does our religion help? It helps by seeking and speaking the truth. Our young ones know when they are being "conned" or manipulated. They have endured hours upon hours of manipulation by television commercials. The church must honestly speak what she has learned. She can no longer presume to speak and have everyone listen. There are too many people and institutions already speaking in our world. It seems that we are being shouted at from all sides about what we should have "faith" in. The church needs a very simple, honest voice, devoid of all aggrandizement. Her priests and teachers will have to admit what they don't know. Otherwise, our children will abandon the church in increasing numbers and they will have every right to do so.

The world of mystery seems to be dying. The light of scientific investigation and rational thought sweeps across everything. That's not always bad. The problem is when we try to explain away everything spoken of a "mystery." Surely love is such a mystery. It will become less and less evident in a world where mystery dies. Our young may be entering a time when mystery will not be enjoyed, but will instead, be ridiculed. Yet if we ridicule mystery, we ridicule both love and God. We also ridicule ourselves, for being human is certainly a mystery.

Religion has to do with mystery, with wonder. As Erich Fromm points out in *Psychoanalysis and Religion*: "One who has not been bewildered, who has never looked upon life and his own existence as phenomena which require answers and yet, paradoxically, for which the only answers are new questions, can hardly understand what religious experience is."

Perhaps that's why so many of our young turn to the East. There they can still encounter a world view which sees the mysterious as sacred. Our Western society has lost a much-needed sense of wonder. Maybe we must all become "pragmatists" in a world that can be destroyed at any time. The threat of nuclear destruction has made us all a bit insane. I think it has also destroyed many of our dreams and visions. We are inclined more to immediate gratifications. We're no longer willing to "put off" for the future, a future which might be swept away with the push of a button.

All around us we hear the possibilities of doom. The potential destruction of humanity is very real. Reading a book like Jonathan Schell's *The Fate of the*

Earth makes us face up to the horror that awaits us if we make a wrong turn. The church will need to become a place of hope, an oasis of *realistic* optimism. She will need to champion humanity's bright side, while never losing awareness of the dark side. The church will need to speak for human potential as she has done in the past. For instance, there are many who argue the need for a moral equivalent to war. Perhaps the church can be in the vanguard of such a search.

When Moses was talking to his people just before they entered the "Promised Land," he said there was a choice laid out before them. They could choose life or death. They could either obey God or turn from him. Moses begged them to "choose life." We, today, are faced with a similar choice. We must also choose between life and death. The choice, though, is not the same as the one made by the Israelites. We're not entering a foreign land, trying to conquer it with force of arms. We're faced with a different kind of foreign territory, the territory of the human heart. We're not out to conquer it at all. We're out to understand it, to explore it.

The last century was an age of great explorations. We went into every corner of the world. We traveled to both the North Pole and the South Pole. We began to explore the deep regions of the oceans. We even went to the moon. It's now time to turn inward, to journey inside of who we are. It's as difficult and as dangerous a journey as any undertaken before. It used to be a journey limited to saints, poets, and mystics. But now it's time for all of us to travel within. Maybe then we can escape the annihilation which clouds our future.

The church can help us to begin. The best way to explore is to have open eyes, not clouded with preconceptions and prejudices. The best way to travel is to travel light. The way we do that is to pack little in the way of assumptions and presuppositions. The church can help us discard what isn't needed. But she will have to discard many things herself. For instance, she will have to dismantle her antiquated and burdensome tribunal system. There are too many priests and other people wasting enormous amounts of time and energy handling marriage cases in the church courts. The church will have to admit the existence of divorce and remarriage. It's not that divorce is desirable. We all know how damaging it can be to the spouses and the children. But for the church to continue requiring annulments prior to remarriage is absurd in a society where half the marriages end in divorce, regardless of religious affiliation. The church cannot hang on to the present system without a great cost in terms of human suffering.

What's the future? I certainly don't know. But I do pray that the church will continue to grow. I pray that the world will survive our nuclear nightmare. I pray that our children will take the time and effort necessary to search within themselves. I pray that we will be able to both see and endure the pain which is all around us. That's asking a lot. Violence seems to be growing by leaps and bounds. I wonder whether any of us feel very happy in a world where the capsule we take for a headache might be laced with cyanide. I wonder whether any of our young will feel safe in a world where their trick-or-treat candy must be x-rayed for razor blades and needles.

Look at one of the theories behind sadism and masochism. I'm not a psychiatrist, so I only offer one explanation as best I understand it. A person who is a masochist finds themselves unable to feel anything unless it is extreme. In other words, they have become so deadened to their feelings, that it takes something extraordinary for them to feel it. So they allow themselves to be beaten or brutalized because at least that they can feel. A similar dynamic, somewhat in reverse, happens in the sadist.

The point is that we are all becoming a bit "deadened." We all see too much too soon. It's like being subjected to continual loud noise. Eventually our hearing will leave us, sometimes gradually, sometimes rapidly. Look at the loss of hearing among our young who habitually attend loud concerts. I remember going once to a parish dance for seventh and eighth graders. I came into the auditorium where a local rock group was playing. I could hardly enter because of the force of the sound. My ears began to ring and I had to quickly make my exit. Yet I saw many of the students gathered up around the loud speakers.

Our feelings are crucial. If we can't feel, then we can't love. It's possible that we're becoming a people unable to love because our feelings have been buried. We are able to attend those modern "mad slasher" movies without blinking our eyes. I recoil in terror when I see so many of our young ones, some even in early grade school, lining up to see the latest serving of blood and gore. It's as if we're needing stronger and stronger shocks to affect us. Like taking prescriptions, we become accustomed to lower doses and have to keep increasing the dosage.

The church needs to be vigorously involved in the struggle to recapture our feelings. The church, along with any religion which wishes to be healthy, must help us learn what it is to feel tenderness, what it is to feel concern. This is especially important if we didn't experience these feelings within our own family.

The church's place is to help us regain our sensitivities, to help us hone the edge of our humanity. If our religion is healthy, it will help us reach out to those who are in pain. If our religion is healthy, it will help us to cry easily and often at what we see, in sorrow and in joy. In other words, while the world seems to keep "hardening" us, healthy religion keeps "softening" us, warming the coldness that can so easily freeze our feelings.

The church needs to help us become vulnerable again, to become again as little children. But, while a child's vulnerability is automatic, an adult's vulnerability can be freely chosen. We can become vulnerable while still understanding, accepting the openness that we so often perceive in our children. But the church will need to show us this vulnerability, this openness, first in herself, by letting us know her doubts and uncertainties. Just as we are turned off by the person who claims to have all the answers, so we will be turned off by a church which claims to have all the answers.

Look at what Kierkegaard said when speaking about religion's purpose: "To strip men of their disguises, to compel them to see evasions for what they are, to label blind alleys, to cut off retreats . . . to enforce self-examination and to bring them solitary and alone before the eternal." In other words, religion's purpose is to make us vulnerable; to ourselves, to our world, and to God. Becoming vulnerable is risky, but the rewards are worth the risks.

A healthy religion also helps us be content with what we have, with the wonders and joys which surround each of us. Television has made us all want too much from life. We see all that we don't have, all the things that could be available if we had the money. But if we want too much, we'll become angry or violent when we don't get it. A healthy religion counterbalances the voracious appetite stimulated by our advertisements and our consumer society.

A healthy religion helps us keep warm when cold winds blow. Otherwise, we will become too "cool." There's something off-kilter in a society that promulgates the "cool" approach to life, the "laid-back" style. Religion helps us to be more on fire. Faith keeps us burning. When we don't have faith, then we are "cool." Faith is the excitement of being alive. Being "cool" is only another form of depression. But for the church to keep us on fire, she must be flaming herself. The one who brings the fire has always been symbolized by the Holy Spirit. When we recall Pentecost, we remember that it was tongues of fire which came down upon the disciples. A healthy religion keeps us in touch with such fire.

I would like to end with a story. One bright summer day, two or three years ago, I was driving from Chicago to Minneapolis. I was traveling along at 55 mph, maybe even a few miles above that. A large monarch butterfly flew in front of my car. I knew that I had hit it. I felt a momentary sadness, asking forgiveness, as I try to do when life is destroyed because of me. I kept driving. I drove for almost another hundred miles when I finally pulled over to a rest stop. I got out and as I was walking by the front of my car, I saw the butterfly caught in my car's grill. I pulled it gently from the grillwork and to my utter amazement, it flew away. I just stood there and wept. I had learned that life is not as fragile as I had imagined. That's really the lesson which healthy religion teaches us.